Keep Calm
and
Parent On

Keep Calm and Parent On

A Guilt-Free Approach to Raising Children by Asking More from Them and Doing Less

EMMA JENNER

Foreword by Debra Messing

ATRIA BOOKS

NEW YORK LONDON TORONTO SYDNEY NEW DELHI

The names and identifying characteristics of the children and families mentioned herein have been changed.

ATRIA BOOKS
A Division of Simon & Schuster, Inc.
1230 Avenue of the Americas
New York, NY 10020

First Atria Books hardcover edition July 2014

Designed by Kyoko Watanabe

Manufactured in the United States of America

10 9 8 7 6 5 4 3 2 1

Library of Congress Cataloging-in-Publication Data
Jenner, Emma.
Keep calm and parent on : a guilt-free approach to raising children by asking more from them and doing less / Emma Jenner.
pages cm
1. Parenting. 2. Parent and child. I. Title.
HQ755.8.J455 2014
306.874—dc23

2013045460

ISBN 978-1-4767-3954-0
ISBN 978-1-4767-3956-4 (ebook)

Contents

CONTENTS

For my mum

Foreword

BECOMING A PARENT.

By far the scariest moment in anyone's life.

Instantaneously transforming from "me" to "we," and being in charge of keeping this vulnerable, beautiful creature ALIVE. It's probably the most overwhelmed I've ever felt in my whole life. I was simultaneously paralyzed with shock and flooded with neurotic, vigilant anxiety that I had NO IDEA OF WHAT I WAS DOING. I was a failure before I had even begun.

(Oh, what we do to ourselves.)

There are so many messages coming at us, as though from passionate campaigning politicians, containing what is supposedly the "right" way to do—well, everything. Whether it's your mother, a coworker, the cashier at the grocery store, or the lady at UPS, *everyone* has an opinion about how to be a good parent; how to raise a healthy, curious, respectful, joyful, independent child. Well meaning as they all are, their suggestions just made me feel more terrified and helpless.

I met Emma Jenner in 2004 when my son, Roman, was three months old. Roman's baby nurse introduced Emma, and she began to work with us on the weekends.

Young, confident, polite, sweet, British—it was Mary Poppins! I joke (kinda) but I can't overstate how important Emma became to my family. What started out as a part-time baby-nurse job turned into a full-time nanny job that took us around the world, from home to hotel, finding schools, meeting and socializing with new friends, experiencing a LOT of change—and Emma was there. We laughed because I called her my wife.

She was my rock.

Through every phase of Roman's development, from a newborn to a six-year-old boy (and even now, still), Emma was my guide. She held my hand (and wiped my tears) during sleep training, had passionate debates with me about "the family bed" and boundaries, threw dance parties to the Wiggles in the living room, and taught me the importance of structure and a schedule. She gave me the strength to be firm when dealing with issues of respect and appropriate behavior, and understood better than most the dispiriting moments of uncertainty that regularly threatened my confidence as a mother. Emma is a passionate advocate for children. She is formally trained and educated; she is smart, wise, and compassionate; funny and playful. She has seen it all. And she is a gift to anyone looking for support and guidance.

I am so happy for all of you who now have access to this very special and talented woman. Keep this book by your bed. It will become your best friend.

And congratulations!

Warmly,
Debra Messing

INTRODUCTION

Fairy Dust

"It's easier to build strong children than to repair broken men."

—Frederick Douglass

I've worked with nannies and parents around the globe, and I've noticed a growing crisis in how children are raised.

Consider this example: An adult enters a room where there is one seat, occupied by a child. Does the child stand and let the adult take the seat? Or if the adult is seated and the child enters, does the adult stand? When I was growing up in Britain in the 1980s, it was unfathomable for a child to sit while an adult stood. And now? It's the opposite. Parents are so eager to make their children comfortable, or to avoid the sounds of their whining, that they sacrifice *themselves*.

I recently overheard a mum asking a dad if he'd gone to the store to pick up bread with their son. "He didn't want to go," said the dad. *He didn't want to go?* My eyes just about popped out of my head. Who was the parent, and who was the child? If this dad could have only heard himself, perhaps it would have been a wake-up call that it was time to regain some control.

Modern parenting is in trouble, and we must understand how we got here before we can make any sense of it. I see four primary causes for our brewing crisis:

1. We've dropped our expectations.

Imagine a raised bar, like a high bar from an Olympics gymnastics competition. We expect our children to surmount this bar. When we were children ourselves, that bar reached our chest level, and to get over it took some effort and discipline, but get over it we did. Gradually, that bar has inched downward. With each passing year we expect less and less of our children. They must merely place a relaxed fingertip on a bar that barely reaches their knee, and we jump for joy. "Daren did the dishes with me tonight!" we say proudly. "What a great kid!" The slippage has been greater in certain countries (sorry, America . . . though in truth, the UK isn't far behind you), but I've yet to see a country or culture beyond reproach.

I once watched while a toddler pulled his father's hair. The dad smiled and removed his son's grip, and the little boy immediately grabbed for a chunk of hair again. The situation was repeated several times. Never did Dad use a stern voice and reprimand him or stop playing with him as a consequence of the rough play. Both the dad and the mum felt their son was too young to behave differently. As another example, I frequently hear parents claim that they can't take their child to a restaurant. "Why not?" I ask. "Because he won't behave. I'm embarrassed and don't want to deal with it." To that I say "Nonsense. He will behave if you expect him to and teach him how." At the end of the day, you have to put in the work, and though it takes time, effort, and patience, it's worth it. I can take an eighteen-month-old, a three-year-old, and a five-year-old into a posh restaurant and know they will behave. How do I know? Because I won't tolerate anything less!

Parents are frequently standing way too close to see their children's capabilities. There's a fairly sentimental car commercial that shows a dad instructing his daughter the ins and outs of driving on a journey she's about to take. When the camera spans to the daughter, she's no more than six—not even capable of reaching the gas pedal. In another shot, she's shown to actually be a teenager, but the point is clear: Parents are inclined to see their children through a special lens, one in which they are always smaller and less capable than they actually are. We are so accustomed to them relying on us for everything, that as that reliance goes away little by little, we are sometimes slow to adjust. On the flip side, we must also set up our children for success and not set the bar unreasonably high. You must understand your child and meet her where she is.

With all of this in mind, I am here to raise the bar. If you take nothing else away from this book, let it be this: **Expect more from your children, and they will rise to it. Expect less, and they will sink.**

2. We've abandoned the village.

Parents do not support one another like they used to; they're too busy competing about whose kids can do better. They don't talk to one another about the struggles they're having—a lost opportunity to get much-needed empathy and perhaps some advice—because they don't want to admit to others when their child misbehaves. Instead of working as a team with other parents and teachers, they're working against one another.

It takes a village to raise a child, and we've lost that village. Though my mum did most of the child rearing in my family, my nana, teachers, the local shopkeeper, and my parents' friends all played a part. In the United States, in contrast, one's parenting style is up for critique by everyone. I would even go so far as to say that most parents are scared to set boundaries in public, for fear someone will judge them.

My friend Abby just told me about an incident at her son's daycare where the teachers were having a difficult time getting her son to eat his yogurt properly without tossing it all about. Abby responded by saying, "Okay, what should I do? Let's fix it." The daycare teachers were shocked that she was so receptive.

Most parents, Abby later learned, would reject any criticism of their child. In contrast, once when I was very young and stole a few penny-sweets from a shop, my mum marched me back and made me apologize to the shopkeeper. If that happened today, in the United States or the UK, the parent might chastise the child, but they'd likely be too embarrassed to admit their child's transgression. My mum was embarrassed, too, no doubt, but it was worth it to teach me a lesson. The bottom line is, without a healthy sense of support and community, parents are on their own trying to do a task that is so much better suited for a village.

3. We take too many shortcuts.

The third problem we face is that parents are harried to such an extent that many take shortcuts wherever they are able. The availability of shortcuts is indeed a blessing in this crazy world, but only if used with care.

The shortcuts I am most opposed to are video games and the TV shows. It will not be news to anyone reading this that our children are too plugged in. Many experts talk about the costs of technology in terms of our children's attention deficit problems, and I agree with this, but the overuse of media causes problems in *many* areas of children's lives. Among other repercussions, it affects their sleep, it affects their schedule, and it affects the rate at which they learn to behave properly. For instance, if you want to attend a baby shower and bring your child, once she acts out, you can plug her into the iPad you brought along instead of doing the harder work of teaching her to conduct herself well in a new setting. It's much easier to ignore poor behavior and give in than it is to teach. But we must resist the easy way and take the longer view!

Another shortcut is food. Perhaps you eat your food on the go, in the car on your way from one engagement to another. Though it is certainly wonderful that such meals are available, the shortcut means that you are losing the opportunity to spend quality time with your children over dinner and to model proper eating habits and table manners.

Shortcuts can be as significant as letting your child watch hours of television, but they can also be as basic as picking up a one-year-old when he falls lightly on his bum (you are in a hurry, and you hate for him to cry) instead of waiting for him to pick himself up. Going for the quick fix saves time and aggravation in the short term, but makes life so much harder in the long term. Think of it as an energy equation. Suppose you want your kindergartner to clean up his room at the end of the day. You could expend twenty minutes and ten units of energy coaxing him to do it or you could clean it yourself in half the time and expend half the energy. True. But you will expend that same energy the next day, and the next. If, instead of cleaning his room for him, you take the extra time and energy to help him do it, in time you will be able to step away completely. And what's more, you'll have created a more responsible human being in the process! If you were running your home like a business, you would never clean the room for him. Though this is a very mathematical way to think of a task, it's extraordinarily helpful when you need to summon those ten units of energy you just don't have.

4. We've lost our sense of proportion.

The fourth and final problem is that we've lost our common sense about moderation in parenting. We have a tendency to overthink parenting, with so many experts and "new" methods and medications, that basic common sense can be elusive. Parents want a quick fix; they want a prescription for how to solve their child's problems, whether it be poor sleep or trouble focusing. But there is no quick fix; there is no new amazing parenting technique that will change your world. There *is*, however, good old common sense. Balance is key and is a huge part of my philosophy. I neither encourage a strict British upbringing nor approve of the overly permissive American style. The solution falls in the middle. Nothing done to an extreme is good, whether it's an all-carrot diet or an all-attachment style of parenting. We are taught that *everything* in moderation is best, so why should parenting be any different? Yet many parents pick the "latest and greatest" parenting theory, then use it to an extreme with their children.

To use an obvious example, consider the firestorm over breastfeeding. Breastfeeding is wonderful, and I wholeheartedly feel that breast is usually best. But not always. There are some mums for whom it is torture, there are some babies for whom it just won't work, and there are some mums who want—no, *need*—the option of supplementing with formula on occasion so that they can sleep for a longer stretch or go out with a friend. In our culture's zeal to promote breastfeeding, we've left moderation completely out of the picture. Many breastfeeding advocates are so fearful that women will see how easy it is to supplement with formula, that they strongly discourage them from ever doing it. Well, guess what? It's not like smoking, where if you have and enjoy a cigarette or two, you have a physical addiction. Let's not be alarmist; let's just arm families with nonbiased information and let them decide what they want to do. Instead of being extreme, let's just use common sense.

A similar exaggeration happens in the language we use with our children. A recent parenting trend has been to avoid the word "no" or any negative-tinged language at all costs, lest it hamper creativity or a child's sense of freedom. Please! Of course, children hear you and do respond better to more positively couched language, so there is a degree to which I'm on board with the philosophy. But sometimes you must say what you mean, and it needs to be something a two-year-old can understand. That word is a simple "no." Getting into psychobabble about feelings will not do you or your child any good.

These four items reveal my fundamental parenting philosophy. You will see echoes of them all over this book. But they are the big-picture canvas, and it is in the details that the real fun begins. To that end, I introduce my checklist.

The Checklist

Each chapter in this book is based around a cornerstone of parenting. I've lived and worked with children in England, Germany, and the United States, with children from their first weeks through their teen years, and with children from the most privileged households in Beverly Hills to those from impoverished communities. Using this background—particularly my international perspective—as a basis, I explain the philosophies undergirding each topic. Then I address questions from a checklist that pertains to that topic.

Most parents know the basics of what they're supposed to do: feed their kids healthy meals, make sure they get enough sleep, show love, and set boundaries. And yet so many still struggle. Their children are disrespectful, badly behaved, perpetually tired, out of control, or demand more energy than parents have. Parents are trying their best, but they're getting stuck. They're simply standing too close to see where.

I have gone into literally hundreds of homes around the world over the years, observed parents with their children, and, by making a few tweaks, have been able to make a significant difference in these families' lives. Parents are shocked how quickly it's possible to improve their children's behavior and the dynamic of their household—as quickly as three days. **Bad behavior is a habit that can be broken.** A child they may have felt was "difficult" or even beyond hope can come around and show respect, manners, and self-control in a way parents never thought possible. (And I always say it can fall apart just as quickly, but more on that later.) I share all of this not to boast, but rather because I feel so strongly about the information in this book, and know there are countless families who could be happier than they are.

The parents I've worked with frequently ask me if I'm sprinkling fairy dust around their children, as if my Britishness means I have Tinker Bell on speed dial. I hate to disappoint them, but no, no fairy dust. (And I won't fly away with my umbrella on the next windy day, either.) Rather, I have my checklist. The checklist brings objectivity back into focus, by asking a series of questions.

When I go into a home, I run through this checklist while I observe the family: How well mannered are the children? What are their eating habits? Where and how does everyone sleep? What kind of schedule is in place? How do the parents handle consequences? Are the adults in the household present and available? These may seem like basic questions, but the more you break them down—and I do—the more you can see how easy the basics are to miss. For example, parents know it's important to give their child consequences when the child misbehaves, but they can lose the energy or the will to be consistent in enforcing those consequences. Parents know unconditional love is crucial, so they may wipe their child's tears while they're disciplining, which sends a mixed message. Parents put a well-balanced meal on the table, but their child sees Mum or Dad fill up on potato chips, or the parent offers cereal when the chicken and peas are rejected. One parent, a teacher, was utterly perplexed that she could control her classroom of twenty-five students, but her four daughters were running her ragged. I have a good friend who was a nanny for years—a much stricter nanny than I am, by the way—and yet all of her rules went out the window once she had her own children.

This blindness by proximity has affected me, too, at times. One little boy I worked with had me stymied as to why he'd been acting out so much lately. Only when I returned from some time away was I able to see the problem: his mum had been really busy meeting a deadline and hadn't been able to spend the quality time with him she usually did. He and I had spent a lot of time together, of course, but he didn't want my attention—he wanted his mum's. Once I saw the problem, it was fairly easy to address. However, because not everyone can leave their charges for a couple of weeks to get a fresh perspective, my checklists can help illuminate the holes.

Parenting is much more like baking a cake than cooking a stew. When you bake a cake, it doesn't matter if you use the highest quality butter when you've forgotten to add the eggs. In the same way, you could read 400 pages about how to handle tantrums and consider yourself a veritable expert yet miss the target completely because in reality, your child isn't getting enough sleep. Or you could read a treatise on nutrition and spend endless effort preparing balanced meals, only for your child to refuse to sit down and eat because you have trouble setting—and sticking to—boundaries. You must see the whole picture together, all the ingredients at once, and the checklist helps you do so.

My checklists will help you get the distance you need to see how you're doing the right things the wrong way, and will help you get back on the right track.

How to Use the Checklists

Use the checklists as a way to imagine me perched on your shoulder watching over you. If your child is having a difficult day, run through the main headings in the table of contents: Sleep? Check. Nutrition?

Check. Consistent limits? Check. Quality time? Check. And so on. Chances are excellent that just in looking at this "list," you'll see that one box is missing its check. It's imperative that you be honest in your answers. You can keep them as private as you like.

You may run through this list daily or even several times a day. While things such as sleep and nutrition are probably in your mind already, my hope is that facets such as quality time and self-esteem will come to be just as natural for you to consider.

If at first glance you can check off every item, then you need to dig deeper. Use the checklists at the beginning of each chapter to help you determine where to focus. For instance, you may get stuck at the "sleep" check mark. You know your child isn't sleeping well, but can't figure out why. You can then go through the entire checklist at the start of the sleep chapter and see where you're being held up.

Finally, the book includes blank checklists in the back. Feel free to pull these out and photocopy. I find it useful to physically mark something off—it gives me a great sense of accomplishment, and it can help visually guide me to where I'm getting stuck.

I've also highlighted tips throughout each chapter. These are practical actions I've found invaluable in my years as a nanny, and I've also included advice from parents. These tips are meant to remind you that you are a part of a community, and it's wonderful and valuable to listen to what's worked for others. They are offered in the spirit of support, not competition.

Though the checklists are simple and meant to be easy to follow, they also represent a deeper philosophy I hope parents will embrace—a reorientation that encourages parents to be in control again, and to thus enjoy their children more. I can't spend three days in every family's home. But with my checklists, you won't need me to. You'll be able to see for yourself where the holes lie, how to fill them, and how to keep them filled.

Parenting is both harder and easier than we think. The checklists in this book will take the guilt and some of the angst out of parenting by putting daily struggles and common problems in objective, systematic terms. Parenting is more art than science, it's true, but there *is* a science to it. And science, in all of its *concreteness*, is comforting. Sometimes science is just what you need on the days when you are at your wit's end and are outnumbered by your darling children who have somehow turned into little monsters. Take a step back, put on your scientist's hat, pull out the appropriate checklist, and investigate.

CHAPTER ONE

The Dignified Parent

For Mum and Dad

"Sacrificing everything for your children isn't selfless, it's ridiculous."

—ELLIE, PLAYED BY BLYTHE DANNER IN THE FILM *THE LUCKY ONE*

CHECKLIST

☑ Are you getting enough sleep?

☑ Are you making time to care for yourself?

☑ Are you making time to care for your relationship with your partner?

☑ Do you greet your spouse first?

☑ Mums: Are you having sex with your partner?

☑ Dads: Are you taking care of Mum?

☑ If there are two parents at home, are you modeling a good relationship to your children in how you treat each other?

☑ Is there joy in the house? Is there a lot of laughter and fun?

☑ Do you enjoy being a parent?

☑ Do you feel confident you can handle your child's behavior?

☑ Are you calm?

☑ Do you ensure that everything does not revolve around the children?

☑ Are you forgiving of yourself when things don't go well?

☑ Are you willing to ask for help?

THERE'S A REASON I chose to make the chapter about taking care of Mum and Dad the first chapter in this book. There's a saying that goes, a family is only as happy as its unhappiest member, and with many families, that member is one of the parents. Parents so rarely put themselves first, and that needs to change for the sake of the whole family.

Parents today are sidelining their own needs in favor of their children's. I know mothers who stop planning girls' nights out once they have a baby and other women who refuse to buy themselves new clothes or splurge on a decent haircut because they want to give everything to their kids. Mums and dads don't expend effort caring for their relationship with each other, and in many households, once the kids come along, they even stop sharing a bed. Their commitment to parenthood is admirable, and yet taking care of themselves, not their children, is the first priority to proper parenting. So, Mum and Dad, here you are, front and center.

There are very tactical reasons this chapter comes first. If you are exhausted, if you are not caring for your own needs, then it will be extremely difficult, if not impossible, to follow through on the checklists in this book. Parenting takes energy—and lots of it. And while I am certain it will take less energy by the time you are done with this book, parenting using my guidelines will take more energy to start with. Find that energy reserve, and find it by making time for yourself.

I know many parents will read that directive and think, "Sure. Would you like to take a look at my schedule and figure out where the space is?" Many parents might even feel that taking care of themselves is a burden and something else that I've added to their crushing to-do lists.

I have two responses:

1. What I'm offering is a more efficient way of operating. You will be more effective if you are rested, you will waste less time, and you will make life easier for yourself—*it's just that simple!*

2. Though finding time for yourself is in part about prioritizing, it's also about *how* you do the things you are already doing. It's a question of emphasis. For instance, when your family gathers for dinner, you may currently be the last one to sit down, and then you may be up out of your chair several times to refill a glass of milk or get your child a second serving of pasta. Why send your family the message that it is less important for you to eat a hot meal than for them? In fact, it's *more* important. In British

> households I'm familiar with, no one gets seconds until everyone is done eating. Your family can wait. The same is true for moments you just need a break and some peace and quiet. If your children are old enough, simply say, "Mummy needs some time for herself right now. Please go play upstairs and I'll be with you shortly."

Before I launch into the checklist, it's worth looking at how we've come to this place where we are ready to pop up and accommodate every need of our child's at every moment. I think there are several culprits.

The first is that we are immersed in a culture of guilt. As more and more families have two parents working, those parents feel they must go home and lock on to everything their child says and does. *Since I get so little time with you*, they reason, *I must be sure you're happy. So what can I do to make you so?* I am a strong proponent of spending quality time with your children, and in fact have devoted an entire chapter in this book to it. **But quality time does not mean meeting your child's every need every moment he has one. Make life easier for yourself, tell him he must wait, and teach him a lesson in patience in the process**.

Adding to our anxiety is the number of parenting experts out there who are serving up guilt like heaping mounds of porridge. Just as the evening news teasers try to get you to tune in by playing on your fears ("Is your home at risk of carbon monoxide poisoning? Tune in at eleven to find out."), experts try to get you to pay attention to their advice by playing on your insecurity. They send message after message about what your kids need to be healthy and happy and balanced, when really a huge part of what your kids need is for *you* to be happy.

A second reason we got here is that we are in the habit of believing our children must be constantly entertained—in part because we ourselves have to be constantly entertained. It starts with the bouncy chairs we put newborns into the first days and weeks of their lives. The chairs vibrate, play music, and offer all manner of shiny objects to amuse the infant. But imagine if you were popped into a chair where you couldn't move, and were forced to vibrate like a Sonicare and listen to tinny music while lights flashed in your face. It sounds like torture! And yet we program our little ones to want such stimulation. Or when they're older, when we pile into the car with our children even for very short trips, we make sure we have snacks and drinks and kid-friendly music. If all else fails, we play games with them. Whatever happened to kids looking out the window and entertaining themselves? We need to teach children to be okay without being entertained at every moment. It's good for them, and it's good for us. It means we can listen to our favorite radio station sometimes, not just theirs. It means we can sit and have a cup of coffee while they play with Lego.

The final factor contributing to our subjugation of self *is* ourselves. I've seen parent after parent fall into codependent relationships with their children. When a parent says something to me like "I can't leave for the weekend because my toddler needs me," I think, "No—you can't leave because you need your toddler." It's healthy for your toddler to learn to be without you. And it's healthy for you to learn to be without her. Half the time when I see parents leaving their children at daycare, the mums and dads draw it out. It's not uncommon for the child to fuss a bit right when his parent goes, but as any daycare teacher will tell you, it lasts for merely a moment, and the best thing to do is to say good-bye to the child quickly with a "Have a fun day, and I'll be back to pick you up later!" But Mum and Dad linger, making it worse for everyone. It's not helpful for the child, so why do they do it?

So let's be aware of and fight these cultural inclinations together. Let's do the work we need to do in order to be happy.

It's fairly easy for someone on the outside (i.e., me) to tell whether a parent is happy or not. It can be harder to see traces of unhappiness in yourself. To that end, honestly answer the following questions:

☑ Are you getting enough sleep?

Everyone needs sleep. Everyone. At the minimum, you need seven or eight hours of sleep per night. If you are not reaching that minimum, consider it the first priority of this book. If you have a newborn, the hours of sleep will not be possible, but do what you must to get rest during the day, and try to get at least a four-hour stretch at night (meaning: wake up your partner if you have one! It's his turn, for heaven's sake).

☑ Are you making time to care for yourself?

You need to take care of yourself. You need nourishing meals, exercise, and time for yourself, even if it's just to relax in a warm bath. You also need friends and people who will support you. When it comes to parenting, nothing else makes sense if the answer to this question is "no," so no excuses.

☑ Are you making time to care for your relationship with your partner?

It's not news to anyone that marriage satisfaction often declines once children enter the picture. Parents don't take time for each other, and often put the kids first. Mum and Dad may be away from their kids so much that they don't want to go out together without them. They may be too exhausted to add one more thing to the calendar, even if it is something enjoyable like a movie or a dinner out. They may not be able to find babysitters easily, or they may not be able to afford them. But if you have a partner, caring for that relationship is a building block for everything else. The more you communicate with each other, the more smoothly your home will run. (More on this in Chapter Two.) The more fun you have together, the lighter everyone's mood will be. Feed the partnership, even if it seems like there's no time. Spend time talking over a cup of tea once the children have gone to bed, or steal off during lunch to spend some time together. Commit to making time together a priority, and notice what a difference it makes.

☑ Do you greet your spouse first?

If you have a spouse, an excellent way to discern how you prioritize that relationship is by how you greet him. If you're not kissing your spouse hello before you kiss your kids, you should. It will not hurt your children's feelings—it merely lets them know that you value Daddy a lot, too, and that that relationship is important. The child's existence likely started with the union between the two of you, so really the whole family should honor its importance.

EMMA TIP

Parents often will trade off babysitting duties with a family in their neighborhood. One week they watch your kids while you go out, and the next week you return the favor. Some families I know even have three families in the rotation, and while one of the couples goes out, the other two families and everyone's kids have a lovely evening together at home. If you're not already part of such a babysitting circle, start one!

☑ Mums: Are you having sex with your partner?

I once led a seminar for a group of new moms. There were eleven altogether, and their babies were between six months and eighteen months. Out of the group of eleven, only one was having regular sex with her spouse. Shocking! If you are not having sex, it's a telltale indication that your union is not being tended to properly.

I understand the aversion. You're tired. If you're nursing, sex might be painful because you'll likely be much drier than usual. You feel like you're taking care of everyone else's needs all the time—you don't want or need sex right now, and if your husband does, too bad for him.

So why do I think you should still do it? Well, first off, understand that I am not suggesting you have sex all the time, or even once a week. And when you're recovering from childbirth, there's a time when you shouldn't be having sex at all. But the women in my seminar hadn't had sex with their partners in months. *Months.* And I know this is a familiar story. It's as though once a baby enters the picture, your own needs and your partner's needs are sidelined, and sex just goes away. I'm not a couples counselor or a sex therapist, but it doesn't take one to know that sex is a way you show your partner love and tenderness. Couples need intimacy, and they need to say through touch, "Hey, you're important to me. Our relationship is important to me." Having a child is going to test you both in so many other ways, you need to make sure your marriage is strong. It's foundational.

If you're not having sex, it may be a strong indication that the

PARENT TIP

Sex was the furthest thing from my mind after my daughter was born, and when my husband and I did have sex, it was pretty painful for a time. But two things helped: (1) K-Y Jelly, and lots of it! And (2) I made sure that I wasn't feeling too run down before a "sex date." I found that the more my husband could help nurture me in other ways (giving the baby a bottle so I could skip a feeding or making me a nice dinner), the more energy I had for him and for our sex life. Believe me, he was more than happy to comply!

little one's needs are overwhelming your needs and those of your spouse. Many mums choose to sleep with their babies (more on this in Chapter Three), but if that's the reason you and your spouse aren't having sex, it's a problem. It's difficult to prioritize intimacy when there's another body in the bed—or even worse, when Mum is sleeping with baby and Dad's in the guest room for nights and nights on end. Sadly, this is a rather permanent situation in many households.

I have an English friend Hannah who was very taken with the notion of attachment parenting, a philosophy that encourages co-sleeping, baby-wearing, and feeding on demand. But if taken to an extreme, such a philosophy negates the *parents'* needs. For example, Hannah slept with her baby girl and nursed her through the night for the entire first year of her baby's life, as well as the entire second year. Hannah's husband, Peter, sometimes joined them, but mostly he slept in the guest room. When Hannah's good friend in America told her she was traveling to Paris and would love to see Hannah and Peter for a weekend there, Hannah said she didn't think she could leave her daughter overnight because she was still nursing. Hannah's friend was worried about her, and gave Hannah a talking-to about how important it was for Hannah and Peter to go out and have fun alone, to have sex, whether it was in Paris or not.

Hannah discussed the possibility of the trip with Peter, who was over the moon about the idea. Seeing how excited he was about it, Hannah agreed they'd go. For the next several weeks, Peter gleefully joked about how he was going to get laid, and referred to it as their "F**k trip to Paris."

☑ Dads: Are you taking care of Mum?

Chances are excellent that even soon after you've welcomed a new baby, your sex drive is still, well, driving. And yet when you suggest it to your wife or partner, she looks or acts put out, maybe incred-

EMMA TIP

For parents struggling to find time to spend alone together, often the problem is the sleep habits of their children. Children need to sleep more than their parents, so there ought to be time in the evenings for Mum and Dad to be alone together. This is one of the many benefits of getting children in their own beds and on a schedule. Often parents feel lost at first when they realize they have an entire evening to themselves. But fear not—I'm sure you can find a way to fill the time if you put your mind to it.

ulous, possibly even offended. Don't give up, but do try a different approach. She is tired, and may feel like she's meeting everyone's needs all day—physical and otherwise—and isn't particularly keen to bother with yours. The best way to meet this reaction is to anticipate it. Make sure *her* needs are taken care of—ensure she's getting proper sleep, some time to herself, and healthy meals that she hasn't necessarily made herself. The more you nurture her, the more room she will have to feel like being sexual again, and the more energy she will have for sex.

☑ **If there are two parents at home, are you modeling a good relationship to your children in how you treat each other?**

I first came to America with a family called the Martins, and though their children are nearly grown now, the family is still a wonderful part of my

PARENT TIP

My husband and I have a date night every week, no matter what, even though sometimes we're tired. We also have a 5:00 to 6:00 p.m. happy hour, which is my son's "witching" hour. He gets to run around and play on his own a bit while we catch up on the day. The glass of wine helps with that last push toward bed!

life. The parents, Wendy and Graham, have an incredible relationship. They are very respectful and present for each other. And their children mimic this, not just in the way they treat their parents but also in the way they treat their significant others. I see the flip side of this role modeling all the time, where the dad might be disrespectful to the mum, or vice versa. The children in turn feel it's acceptable to be disrespectful to their parent, or other people they care about. When Mum and Dad aren't nice to each other, typically the entire vibe of the household is hostile. It is hard for anyone—parents or children—to be happy in such an environment.

☑ Is there joy in the house? Is there a lot of laughter and fun?

For some parents, it's easy to be playful. Others—probably the majority, really—are so focused on their to-do list or cleaning up messes or getting on with their evening that they forget to treasure the moments, to remember that the days may be long but the years are short. You must get into the habit of putting aside tasks and chores, putting on music, and dancing. You must allow your children to be silly and make faces and laugh and be utterly free. And you must do it, too. It makes your children feel secure when they see you feeling happy, and when they are allowed to be happy as well.

☑ Do you enjoy being a parent?

You will not always be happy, and that's okay. There are times when you feel overwhelmed, and that's okay, too—you're human! But how often do you feel this way? More than occasionally? More often than you don't? I see many mums, in particular, who are depressed. It may be because they've buried their own needs so deeply that they don't even realize how long it's been since they've laughed. It may be lingering postpartum depression. It may be a long-standing physiological problem that they are not tending to. Here's how I spot a depressed mum or dad: They don't touch their kids. They don't smile. They slouch. Their eating habits are odd—either they eat too much or too little. There is no bounce or energy to their movements. Their tone is short and snappy and they just generally seem pissed off at the world.

If you think you might be depressed, you owe it to yourself and to your family to address the issue. If the depression is serious, it may involve visiting your doctor. If you're just feeling a bit down, you may be able to pull yourself out of it by going for a walk by yourself, giving yourself some relief. You may be surprised at how quickly the picture will change. Think about it from the child's perspective. If his mum never laughs with him or smiles or tickles him, how does that feel? If each time he asks a question, his parent snaps at him, how must that feel? How must that affect his own behavior? When you consider it this way, it's clear how your own well-being is critical to a harmonious home.

☑ *Do you feel confident you can handle your child's behavior?*

If you feel confident you can handle your child in any situation, you will not fear her or her behavior, and you will embrace your days with far less stress. There is a surefire way I can determine whether a parent is confident or afraid. I call it the Sippy Cup Test. Imagine this familiar scenario: It's breakfast time, and little Miranda has asked for some milk. You pour it into a blue sippy cup, and Miranda's eyes widen. "Noooo!" she cries, "I want the pink sippy cup!" Do you

a. tense up and scramble for the pink sippy cup so that you can avoid a Miranda meltdown before you've even had coffee, or

b. calmly say, "I've already poured your milk into the blue sippy cup this morning, but if you remind me at lunchtime, you can have your milk in the pink cup then."

If you answered b, congratulations! You passed. It is true that at first, the child may melt down, and we will go into this more in Chapter Seven when we talk about boundaries and consequences. But the confident parent does not fear meltdowns. The confident parent knows that it's silly to make more work for herself; who wants to wash two sippy cups instead of one? **Don't let your child rule the roost or stop you from doing something. Know that you can handle whatever she throws your way because you are the parent, and she is the child.** When you know this, it gives you a great sense of control. There's nothing worse than feeling powerless and at the mercy of your child and your child's meltdowns.

☑ Are you calm?

This can be a magical fix. One parent I know was at the end of her rope after the whole family had been ill. She'd had no time for self-care or rest. When her preschooler became too difficult, the mum jumped into the bathroom to collect herself. When she opened the bathroom door a few minutes later, she smiled brightly and spoke in a calm voice (even though she was not yet feeling exactly that way). Almost like magic, the preschooler settled down. In reality it wasn't magic at all, but a voice that was just less edgy than it was before, and a smile instead of a knotted forehead. Being calm shows children that you're in control and everything's okay. Kids feel anxiety, and it in turn makes them anxious. For all these reasons, it's appropriate to give *yourself* a time-out when you need a break from parenting!

EMMA TIP

Learn to recognize signs that your child's behavior is affecting you. Are you rattled? Are you tight? Is your voice harsh? Make sure your child is safe, and walk into another room or just outside the door. Who cares if she's having a tantrum? **Let her behavior affect her, not you.** Take ten deep breaths of air. Stretch. Perhaps call a friend to vent if that helps you. It's liberating when you recognize that disengaging from a stressful moment, even if just for a moment, can change the tenor of your evening, as well as your child's.

☑ **Do you ensure that everything does not revolve around the children?**

A friend recently asked me for advice about caring for her newborn and her toddler. "What do I do if they're both crying at the same time?" she asked. The answer is obvious: one has to wait. But what is much more interesting to me about this question is that she asked it in the first place. This friend had recently joined a support group for second-time mums, and nearly everyone in the group had this same question. The question reveals how much our parenting mind-set has shifted—we cannot bear to let our children be uncomfortable. But we cannot possibly make them comfortable all of the time. With a single child, it may be manageable (although I would argue too much work and unnecessary!), but with two, it certainly is not. Most important, it's not good for children to get whatever they want whenever they want it.

It drives me mad when I hear new mums talk about how they can't even take a shower. Of course they can take a shower! They need to! If no one is around to care for the baby, pop him in a bouncy chair in the bathroom with you. You can still sing to him and talk to him from the shower. If he cries for a moment or two, he will be fine. In fact, it's important for him to cry. As we'll discuss in Chapter Three, hearing your child cry is an important part of *learning* your child's cry.

This distress about our children's comfort starts when they're newborns, and carries on until they're much, much older. When they're four and you're at the zoo and they want something to drink, you drop everything in order to get them some juice immediately, lest they be thirsty. When they're ten and they refuse to eat their dinner, you let them eat a snack at nine o'clock, lest they be hungry. We must learn to let our children be uncomfortable sometimes. Imagine a twenty-five-year-old job candidate who has never had to wait or experience discomfort. Does he really have the skills to succeed? Does he fully understand the world is not oriented around him? If that's not enough incentive to be a little more self-focused, just think of the undue pressure you are putting on yourself each time your children say "Jump" and you ask "Okay, how high?"

☑ Are you forgiving of yourself when things don't go well?

Part of taking care of yourself means being kind to yourself. Parenting is hard. You will always feel like there's a way you could be doing it better, just as there's always one more load of laundry you could toss in or one more house project to do. I've cried in frustration in front of children I've been caring for. And though it's true I've taught many children to behave well, I've failed completely when it comes to teaching my dog! I let my little six-pound fluffball of a pooch run circles around me! It all goes to show that it's just so much harder to manage when the problems are so close to you.

If you are one of those parents who takes every setback deeply to heart and stays up at night thinking of ways you could have done it differently, do yourself and your children a favor and relax. It's okay for them to know you're human. It's actually a wonderful thing for them to see.

Now, imagine this scenario: You've had a hellish day and the kids are spiraling out of control. Your spouse has just called to say he has to work late, so it looks like you're on duty for another several hours, and you're exhausted. Do you

a. go through your routine as normal, making a home-cooked dinner and insisting on bath time, or

b. cut yourself some slack? Mac and cheese will do just fine tonight, and the kids can bathe tomorrow.

The correct answer is b. Part of being kind to yourself means letting go of your high standards when you need to. You need a break—give yourself one.

☑ Are you willing to ask for help?

We have gotten way too absorbed in what other people think of our parenting. We give a child a lolly to keep him from making a scene, because we just know the checkout clerk will think our child is a terror and we are a horrible parent if we allow him to tantrum. We are too restrained about saying to other mums and dads, "This is really hard," because we don't want them to think we can't handle it, or that our child is less than great. It used to be that parents supported one another, and communities pitched in to help mums and dads when they felt in over their head. Now we're all parenting in isolation and putting on our rosiest public faces for one another. This must stop.

> PARENT TIP
>
> When I'm at my limit, I pour myself a sparkling water with a lime or lemon, which feels like a mini-vacation.

Learn to ask for help. Start by being honest with your friends about your tough spots, and encourage them to be honest with you. Find the ones who are the most open about the difficulties and build on those relationships. And if you see a mum struggling with a tantruming toddler, give her a reassuring smile and tell her you've been there and that you understand. **She is actually a better parent for letting her child cry than for filling his mouth with a lolly.** Self-care and strong parenting starts with supportive communities, and we can all play a part to make our communities more honest and less judgmental.

A Few Words About Baby Shaking

We rarely address what's known as baby shaking unless people are huddled around sordid related newspaper headlines. The subject is taboo. But I want to change that. People need to talk about their frustrations with their babies. Particularly for new mums, it's not socially acceptable for them to discuss any feelings of ambivalence about motherhood, but they need to. Having a solid support network that does not judge anything they say can go such a long way toward helping mums feel better.

We need to be more honest about how hard parenting is. Nobody ever prepares you for how rough it can be. In part that's because it can be tricky to explain, and people are prone to amnesia about those early weeks. And in part it's because there's a national dialogue that celebrates birth and babies as simply wonderful, and leaves no room for the parts that aren't so wonderful. Instead, it's a competition about who's happiest, who's most content. We need to make it okay for parents to call up one another and say, "This is really hard. In fact, it sucks right now." We need to make it okay for mums to say, "I know I will be a great mum, but I'm not that excited about infants." We need to be honest with each other.

I also think people need to feel empowered to let their babies cry. I am not suggesting you neglect your newborn; comforting him regularly is very important to his sense of security and attachment.

But when you are alone with your baby, and he has been crying for what feels like hours on end, and you have tried everything and are at your wit's end, put him down. Leave the room. Take deep breaths. Call someone. Remember that it's only human to be frazzled sometimes by a baby. Don't be so afraid of letting him cry alone that you subject yourself to madness.

This is not a socioeconomic or cultural issue. A friend of mine who was herself a nanny for years and years confided in me that though she knows she wouldn't shake her baby, now that she's been in the situation of trying to console a screaming infant, she can see how it happens. Another parent of three, though her children are all grown, still vividly remembers feeling like a failure when her babies cried. She was frightened by how she was spiraling out of control. How could it be possible that she was having these terrible thoughts and all she wanted from the babies she so deeply loved was for them to shut up? **Having these feelings did *not* make her a failure.** When you are that exhausted and frustrated, it doesn't take much to send you over the edge. In other words, baby shaking can easily happen to the best of us, and we are especially vulnerable to it as a society if we keep quiet about the issues that lead to it.

We also need to remind parents that some infants are particularly tough, but that does not mean they are "bad" babies. There's too much judgment in that label. There are too many mums who look wistfully at other babies who seem to coo and cuddle nicely, while their baby seems to do nothing but scream. The reality is, some babies have colic or gas or a variety of other issues that make them fussy. And so do some toddlers, and so do some grade-schoolers, and so do some preteens, and on and on. Every child goes through a difficult spell. But they will grow out of it. Remind yourself to take the long view.

CHAPTER TWO

The King's Speech

Communication

"The single biggest problem with communication is the illusion that it has taken place."

—George Bernard Shaw

CHECKLIST

☑ Are tantrums infrequent rather than often?

☑ Does your child listen at home as well as he does at school?

☑ Does your child hear and pay attention to your requests?

☑ Do you say the seven most important things? (I love you, I'm sorry, Yes, Stop, Please, Thank you, I know you can do it)

☑ Are you specific about the behavior you want, or don't want, and why? Have you explained the consequences?

☑ Are you communicating the behavior you want ahead of time?

☑ Do you avoid commands?

☑ Do you tell your child what to do rather than ask?

☑ Does your word choice place the responsibility on your child?

☑ Do you say it like you mean it?

☑ Are you avoiding tones that are too strong?

☑ Are you physically near your child and making eye contact when you're making a point?

☑ Is your body language sending a consistent message with your words?

☑ Are you communicating about transitions?

☑ If your child is very young—a baby or young toddler—do you talk to him and assume he's able to understand? Do you tell him what's happening and why?

☑ Are you offering choices?

☑ Are you using concepts and language that are age appropriate?

☑ Do you avoid repeating a request ad nauseam?

☑ Is your child able to talk to you? Do you hear her, listen to her, and respond?

☑ Are you reading your child's body language?

☑ Do you wait until your child is calm before communicating with her?

☑ Are you encouraging your child to use his words instead of whining or crying?

☑ Are the adults in your child's life consistent with one another?

A GUY I USED to work with could really get my knickers in a twist. When I'd go home seething after an encounter with him, I'd often stop myself and think, *Emma, what is the problem? What did he actually say that's got you so bothered?* Reflecting on his words, on what he wanted from me, I'd see it really wasn't bad at all. But he had a way of communicating with me that drove me nuts. He would phrase things in such a condescending manner, or take an imperious tone that immediately made me not want to do a thing for him.

Most readers can probably relate. Countless leadership and relationship books and workshops focus on communication, how important it is, and how easy it is to get it wrong. If it were a simple matter, these scores of books and seminars would not exist! **We put loads of energy into our communication style when it comes to business and marriage, but not many see that communicating with our children requires similar attention.**

The first bit of good news in this chapter is that the results of good household communication are easy to see—there's tremendous opportunity for instant gratification. The second is that I'm not recommending you turn the bus around so much as make a series of *tweaks*. Chances are good you're already communicating with your children in some way, and if it's not effective, sometimes all it takes is a small change to get the results you want. For instance, I worked with a dad who was saying all of the right things, but there was no control or authority in his voice, so his son tuned him out. I made him practice that tone: controlled and confident. And I've worked with a mum who said the right things in the right tone, but her back was turned and her daughter didn't grasp the importance of the command. All we needed to do was turn Mum around. And all too frequently, children receive mixed messages from their parents, rendering even the best communication from one parent moot because the parents aren't talking to *each other*. Or the child will receive a mixed message from the same parent, who is hugging him and wiping away his tears even as she's trying to discipline. Small tweaks can fix all of these communication breakdowns.

I could not write an effective parenting book without a chapter about communication. Without good communication, *how* are you to handle the chapters that follow on sleep, eating, and manners? Communication runs through each chapter to come. It is intrinsic to your success. At its core, how parents communicate with their children and how children communicate with their parents is a window into the level of respect family members have for one another. While at first it may take you some effort to change long-standing habits in word choice, tone, and body language, good communication *will* become second nature. And it will make a miraculous difference, just like you're sprinkling fairy dust.

☑ Are tantrums infrequent rather than often?

Tantrums are a huge telltale sign that communication is off. Of course, every child will have tantrums, and just because yours has one does not mean you have terrible communication. But if a child is having many tantrums, it can be an important sign. Why are they having those tantrums? Are they looking for attention? Are they frustrated? Are they unable to express themselves? If so, why? Read on, and let's see if we can figure it out, shall we?

☑ Does your child listen at home as well as he does at school?

If parents ask for my help because life with their child at home is a nightmare, I usually ask to watch how the child behaves at school. Is he listening there? If the answer is no, there's a bigger problem that needs addressing. If the answer is yes, he clearly can behave but is choosing not to do so at home for his parent. Then it becomes clear that something is off at home. This information is critical, because it focuses my investigation onto what's happening at home and why.

☑ Does your child hear and pay attention to your requests?

I watch to see if a child responds to his parents when they speak to him. Sometimes, if he doesn't respond, it's a simple matter of him literally not hearing. Perhaps Mum has shouted from downstairs while little Billy has music on in his room. That's an easy enough problem to fix. But "does your child pay attention?" is much more fraught, as knows any parent who has thought, *If I have to tell her one more time to put on her coat, I'm going to burst!* The first key here is having reasonable expectations. No kid is going to listen 100 percent of the time. If they sit when you ask them to 80 percent of the time, say thank you

> **EMMA TIP**
>
> If your children could use some help with their listening skills, you might play the classic "telephone" game with them. Have the whole family sit in a line, and the person on one edge whispers a word to the person sitting next to him, and the word is passed down to the end, at which point it's said aloud to see if it's the same word that was started with. Even though children today may not know what a telephone is (a cell phone, sure), they still delight in this game.

when you ask them to, great. You probably will never get to 100 percent, and that's okay.

Know, too, that if you tell your four-year-old to please dress herself for school, you *will* have to keep on her. Simply telling her to put her clothes on may not be enough. Schedules help, as we'll discuss in Chapter Six. It will also help to make sure that what you're asking is something she's capable of. Perhaps start with just asking her to take off her pajamas, something you've seen her do a thousand times and know she can do easily. Then you might say, "I know you want to play with all of your other things, but you're doing nothing—absolutely nothing—until you are dressed and ready." When you see her wandering, say, "Focus!" and help jolly her along.

Assuming, however, that the task is appropriate for her development and she's receptive as you move her along, there may be other reasons she's tuning you out. The rest of these checklist questions will help you narrow down what they are.

EMMA TIP

Instead of always sounding strict, I sometimes make light of a child not listening. I'll say, "Oh no, Jack isn't listening. Where have his ears gone?" And he'll say, "Emma, they're here, look!" as he grasps on to his ears. Then I say, "Fantastic! I was worried you had lost them or left them at school. Now that you've found your ears, can you please come and sit at the table?" Sometimes I'll switch it up and worry that perhaps the child has broccoli growing in his ears—why else wouldn't he be able to hear me? Children love this, and it gets them to focus on the act of listening.

☑ Do you say the seven most important things?

There are seven critical phrases I listen for from parents, as they convey a world of meaning:

1. "I love you"

Take note, Brits! Americans are much better at saying "I love you." Americans seem to grasp that unconditional love cannot be taken for granted, that it's something we need to express to one another. Children need demonstrations of your love in order to feel safe and to flourish. Show it, say it, *communicate it.*

2. "I'm sorry"

There are going to be days when you will snap at your child. Any parent who says she never snaps isn't being truthful. It happens, and it's okay, but you must apologize. "I'm really sorry that I reacted the way that I did," you might say. "I'm feeling tired today and it wasn't your fault. I bet it hurt your feelings when I snapped at you." "I'm sorry," is such a powerful expression because it models empathy and accountability, and it lets your child know you aren't perfect, and it's okay not to be perfect. Human beings are flawed, and that's normal. Some children need to hear this more than others. *They* don't always have to be perfect, either.

3. "Yes" (more than "no")

If someone constantly says "no" to you, you learn to tune them out. We are plainly wired to want to hear "yes" more than "no," and to respond accordingly. If you often say the word "no" to your child or "you cannot do x, y, or z," then your child will cease to hear you. Whenever possible, say "yes" instead, even if the desired behavior is the same. For example, if your child asks if he can play with something but it's nearly dinnertime, say, "Yes, absolutely you can play with that, after we have dinner." If you say no—and don't get me wrong, "no" is a very important and powerful word they are bound to hear often in their lives and need to grasp—then give a reason: "No, you can't touch the oven because it's hot and could burn you."

4. "Stop" (to protect)

A family I worked with lived on a lovely side street next to a busy road. One of the family's young daughters made a habit of running to the road and did not register the word "stop" when her parents shouted it. This was a huge problem, as "stop" is a critical word for keeping a child safe. You must not overuse it, and when you do, you must ensure it always gets immediate results.

> **EMMA TIP**
>
> A fun way to teach the association of "stop" with the act of freezing is to play music and dance around with your child. When you stop the music, you both stop dancing. For a more practical application, every time you come to a street crossing, stop and say "stop" or "red light."

5. "Please"

As we'll discuss in Chapter Five, on manners, saying "please" shows your children respect, and it models the way you want them to speak to others, including you!

6. "Thank you"

Saying "thank you" to your children allows them to feel acknowledged and seen. It emphasizes the importance of gratitude, and reinforces the behavior you want to see. If you don't say "thank you" when they do something well, such as clearing their plate without being asked, they will start to believe they are only noticed when they behave badly.

7. "I know you can do it"

Let's assume your preschooler is embarking on her first swim class. As she lines up with the other children, she looks at you anxiously. You have a choice about how to respond. You can either

a. mollycoddle her, protective of the anxiety she's feeling;

b. communicate confidence in her through your words and body language;

c. tell her not to be afraid, that there's nothing to be scared of and she needs to just dive in.

B is of course the correct answer. "I know you can do it" instills your child with confidence, it reinforces independence, and it's encouraging. It is the best compromise between answers a and c. It acknowledges her anxiety while still building her up. The combination is powerful.

☑ Are you specific about the behavior you want, or don't want, and why? Have you explained the consequences?

Once when I was about three, I was running about the house naked when my mum told me to get ready because we were going out in the snow. I went to my room and "got ready," or so I thought. I showed up at the front door ready to venture out. I was wearing my hat, scarf, and gloves, but otherwise was buck naked. It's a favorite family story, but it has an important point. You must be specific with children—much more than you may realize. You cannot speak to them in shorthand the way you would to an adult. You can't simply say, "Get ready" or "Don't touch that" and presume they know what you're talking about. To that end, I encourage parents to get into the habit of communicating the following:

1. **What.** Let them know they can't do X, and be specific about what X is. Don't say, "Don't touch that"— say, "Don't touch the stove." If it's a behavior you *want*, you might say, "Please get your pants, socks, shoes, and shirt on."

2. **Why.** Explain "The stove is hot and can burn you" or "Please get dressed because we're going to leave for school."

3. **Consequences.** Children will be more likely to cooperate if they know what will happen if that behavior isn't present. So as you take out Play-Doh, for example, you might say, "The Play-Doh needs to stay on the table. If the Play-Doh leaves the table, you are going to have to clean it up and put it away for the day."

I see so many parents saying simply, "Don't do that!" One dad I helped used to shout at his kids at the dinner table all the time, but there weren't any concrete rules the children were aware of. One child would be throwing his food, and the dad would say, "Cut it out!" Another would be making noise with his silverware, and the dad would say, "Stop that!" He was just shouting, really; he wasn't explaining what rule they weren't following, and why they couldn't do the amorphous *that*. He should have said, "Billy, don't throw your food because it's terrible manners and makes a mess. If you throw your food one more time, then I will take your food away."

Or take a common example at the park: If Brenda throws sand at another child in the sandbox, don't simply say, "No!" Instead say, "Brenda, do not throw sand at Red. It could get into his eyes and really hurt him. You can fill your bucket up with sand, but if you throw sand at Red one more time, you are going to have to leave the sandbox." If your child is older and can talk, have her repeat the expectation back to you so you know she understands. And then, if your child plays nicely after you've explained the behavior you want, let her know how happy you are that she played nicely in the sand. This will encourage her to listen to you and to behave. **Remember, kids want to please you.**

☑ Are you communicating the behavior you want ahead of time?

EMMA TIP

Involve your child in communicating the behaviors you want. Discuss them with her and make a sign with her that you put on the refrigerator or somewhere obvious. Have her decorate it and even choose where to put it. Use it as a reminder for the behavior you want not just from your child but also from yourself!

Get into the habit of communicating the behavior you expect from your child and why *before* a particular event. If you haven't established an expectation, and then you overreact when the child doesn't follow it, it's confusing to him—he wasn't born with an innate ability to make good choices. Before a birthday party, dinner party, or trip to the grocery store, be clear about what you want, and in positive terms. This is an incredibly effective way to set up your child for success. So you might say, "We're going into a restaurant in a minute and I expect you to sit down nicely at the table. I want your legs to stay under the table, please, and I expect you to use your manners and to eat your dinner nicely."

EMMA TIP

Avoid using negative terms and behaviors when preparing your child for an event. As a general rule, don't say, "I don't want you running around and screaming in the restaurant," which might just put that bad behavior in his head. But if your child is particularly prone to running around and screaming in restaurants, then you might need to call out in advance the negative behavior and its consequences: "Under no circumstances are you to be running around and screaming, and if you do, we'll leave the restaurant." If you explain this consequence, make sure you are prepared to follow through, and also that leaving the restaurant is not your child's ultimate objective, in which case he'll have won the day!

EMMA TIP

Just as timing is critical to setting up your child for the behavior you want, it's also critical to stopping the behavior you don't want. You must deal with negative behavior as it happens. If your child is whining in a store, don't wait until you are in the car to tell her it wasn't acceptable. Tell her right there in the store, although if you are with others, take her aside and do it quietly and privately, so as not to embarrass her.

☑ *Do you avoid commands?*

Most every parent is guilty of giving commands, like "Get dressed," "Brush your hair," "Clean up these toys," and "Stop that." Commands are strong phrases uttered usually in frustration or anger. Think back to your most recent weekday morning. As you got the kids dressed, the dog fed, the lunches made, and the house picked up, you likely felt more like a field commander than a loving parent. Perfectly understandable, as when you are balancing a flurry of tasks within a time crunch, your primary objective is keeping everyone focused. The problem is that when children hear commands, they feel defensive. They are less likely to respond to your request, and are more likely to argue with you, slowing everything down and ratcheting up the tension in the household. So the next time you are trying to get everyone out of the house, be aware of your tone and phrasing. It takes a mere second longer to add the word "please" and it takes no longer at all to change the tone you're using. Notice what a huge difference it makes. My bet is that you will get out of the house faster, and with fewer arguments. Save the commands for when you really need them, for when you're at the end of your tether and really must get out of the house immediately. If you use commands infrequently, they will hold more power when you need them most.

☑ Do you tell your child what to do rather than ask?

I've watched enough American crime dramas in my time to know that one of the cardinal rules of cross-examination is "Don't ask a question you don't already know the answer to." Parents can take a tip from *Law & Order* on this front. Do not ask, "You need to go brush your teeth, okay?" because that leaves your child free to say, "No, that's not okay." Instead say, "Please go and brush your teeth." After all, you wouldn't say, "Can you hold my hand while we cross the road?" It's clearly not a question, but an instruction.

However, if you really do have a question, such as "Would you like to help me bake a cake?" it's fine to ask, but be prepared for them to say "No," and to be okay with it. It's a small tweak, really, as many parents get in the habit of asking when they should be telling.

☑ Does your word choice place the responsibility on your child?

Like tone, changing your phrasing takes no extra time but makes all the difference. Instead of saying, "I need you to help me clean this up," say, "Do you need my help cleaning this up?" With the latter, you've made the responsibility theirs, not yours. The same trick of language can be used when disciplining. Instead of "Please clean up your room," you might say, "Your room is a mess—what is your plan?" You always want to make your child do the thinking. When you make him part of the plan, when you give him the responsibility, you give him some of the power. He is more likely to cooperate.

☑ Do you say it like you mean it?

Whenever I tell a child he needs to do something, I know he is going to do it. This assurance comes across in my voice. That doesn't mean that I am sure he will respond, "Of course, Emma! My pleasure!" Rather, it means I know that even if I have to help him move his body or limbs in order to make it happen, it will happen. And my confidence comes through in my request. I've heard mums and dads say to their kids, "Honey, please go sit on the toilet before we leave for the playground" in such a way that I can tell they're holding their breath, hoping that the child will do it without an argument. Perhaps there's an upward lift in the parent's voice, such that even if they are not asking a question, it seems like they are. Or perhaps the parent's voice is too soft. They are planning to relent if the child refuses, and the child can *tell*. Children are brilliant at reading tones. If, however, Mum or Dad is certain that one way or another, that child *will* sit on that toilet before leaving, it comes through. The same is true for ending undesirable behavior. "Oh, please don't splash water, honey," becomes "No. You mustn't splash water because it's making a mess."

In short, you must own it. You must know you are the parent, and your children are going to do as you say, and if they don't, you will deal with it. You are not afraid of them having a meltdown, because you know you'll be able to handle it. All of this and more comes across in your vocal inflection.

☑ Are you avoiding tones that are too strong? (yelling)

Just as children sense weakness in tone, they learn how to tune out yelling. One family I worked with never spoke normally to one another; they only yelled. They yelled about things that mattered and things that didn't. The mum used to take Tylenol like crazy because she had a constant headache from all the yelling. The entire family needed to turn down the volume. They had forgotten how to listen, and so their tactic was to keep turning up the noise level in the hopes that someone might pay attention to them. After an hour in their home, I was ready to run for the hills and take a nap.

In another family, the dad—who was really an excellent dad, by the way—had this habit of barking at his children. He loved them dearly, but he thought that the drill sergeant approach was the one that would make his sons respect him. Untrue. It just led to the boys feeling defensive, and occasionally withdrawing completely. They didn't listen to Dad, and so he barked more. Like the yelling family, it had become a habit, a standard of behavior.

Being wishy-washy and weak is no good, as we've discussed, but being too forceful doesn't work, either. You must be calm, confident, and in control. Yelling shows you're out of control, and kids can sense that. Remember the mum in Chapter One who composed herself in the bathroom and came out to a much calmer child? When children sense their parent is stressed, they are apt to act out more, not less. When children sense their parent is calm, the opposite is true.

☑ Are you physically near your child and making eye contact when you're making a point?

It's truly stunning what a difference physical proximity makes. If you have a point to make with your child, do not do so from up on a step stool or from another room. Crouch down to her level, so that you are meeting eye to eye. Ask her to look *at you* as well. If your child is under three, she may not be able to look into your eyes yet, but by the time she's four, she should be capable of maintaining eye contact. This does not mean that every time you say, "Would you like Cheerios or toast for breakfast?" that you need to walk across the room and get on your child's level. But for important discussions, for saying "no," or just for getting a child to cooperate with you on a particularly uncooperative morning, you must meet children where they are—and often that's approximately at the three-foot-high mark.

☑ Is your body language sending a consistent message with your words?

When disciplining or making an important point, touch your child in an affirming way, but do not cuddle her. Be mindful of sending clear messages with your words and body language. It won't work at all to be cuddling and kissing your child as you are letting her know that her behavior was unacceptable. I know it's hard to refrain from wiping tears—and you certainly can wipe those tears away in a bit—but you must focus on one thing at a time. First comes the discipline, and it must stick. Don't confuse the importance of your words by linking them with love and affection. Mixed messages may make the child think that when he acts out and hits his brother, he gets cuddled, so long as he's crying.

☑ Are you communicating about transitions?

It's often difficult for young children to move from one event to the next, which makes sense if you stop and think about it. You're the one calling the shots, and they're pretty powerless. Imagine how you'd feel if you were eating your breakfast and reading the paper, and suddenly someone came in and picked you up out of your seat and said, "Off to work with you! Good-bye!" You'd be furious. You need time to adjust from one activity to another, and children are no different.

If your child is just learning to talk, help her transition by giving her a bit of control, and showing her the words to use. You might say, "Would you like to have one more minute to play before we leave? How do you ask that instead of throwing your body on the floor?" For older children, you may need to be more firm. If it's nearly bedtime but you can see your son's engrossed in his trains, say, "Five more minutes, and then we're going to have a bath." Then alert him when he has just one minute left. Similarly, if a child is used to a certain schedule, and it's changing, communicate the change: "We're not going to the park this morning like we usually do because we have a doctor's appointment. After you play here for a bit, we're going to go to the doctor's appointment and you can bring your special bear to play with in the waiting room. Then we're going to come back home for lunch." Communicate about transitions, give children time to switch gears, and you'll avoid a lot of meltdowns.

> PARENT TIP
>
> If we're about to transition from one thing to the next, I often set a timer for two minutes and tell them, "You have two more minutes to play, so play hard! Then when the timer goes off, it's time to go!"

☑ **If your child is very young—a baby or young toddler—do you talk to him and assume he's able to understand? Do you tell him what's happening and why?**

One of the more common mistakes parents make is to underestimate their children's comprehension. I've seen one-year-olds stand up in the bathtub, and when Dad says they need to sit down because it's not safe to stand, they sit. Communicate with similar clarity about what you're doing with your baby. Think about how powerless you would feel if you were them. Even for very young children, parents should say, "I'm going to change your diaper now because it's dirty," or "We're going to the grocery store so we can get food," or "I'm going to pick you up now." Talk constantly, and give them a chance to understand you. They will develop an association between your words and actions.

☑ Are you offering choices?

Just as children want to know when they're coming and going, as it gives them more of a sense of control, they also want choices. In fact, offering them a choice is a brilliant way to communicate what's happening, at the same time that you're sharing some power. You might say, "Do you want broccoli or green beans with your dinner?" "Would you like to brush your teeth before you get into your pajamas or after?" For most children, anything more than two choices is overwhelming, so keep it at two.

☑ Are you using concepts and language that are age appropriate?

In the sketch comedy *Portlandia*, eager parents sit their four-year-old down and explain to him why they feel it's important for him to get into the best preschool. They show him a detailed chart of his life if he gets into the preschool—including things like an Ivy League degree, a well-paying job, and a particular type of car. Then they show him a visual of what his trajectory will look like if he does not get into the school. There are many funny things about the skit, but foremost among them is the fact that the charts are so complex and so clearly over the child's head. Though it's satire, satire comes from truth, and parents often expect children to grasp concepts that are completely beyond them.

Let's assume your four-year-old daughter is clearly overtired from celebrating her birthday, and you sense she is also disappointed that the party is over and she's no longer the center of attention. Regardless of the cause, she is being rude and disrespectful to you. Do you

a. ignore the behavior and walk away,

b. have an extended conversation about her feelings and your feelings,

c. tell her you understand she's not happy right now, but that she needs to spend some time alone until she's ready to apologize for her behavior?

The correct answer is c. Don't ignore affronts to respect. Don't get into a feelings-oriented conversation that is more appropriate for an episode of *The View* than for a four-year-old. It's great to say, "You're disappointed. I get that. But you still mustn't be rude to mummy." But that's it—save the rest of the feelings talk for when she's a teenager and keep it simple.

☑ Do you avoid repeating a request ad nauseam?

Please forgive me for comparing children to dogs for a moment, but there is an excellent principle used in dog training that is equally effective for kids. If you tell your beloved terrier to "Come!" and he doesn't, and so you again say "Come!" and then say it yet again, he learns to tune you out. He doesn't need to come when you call because you'll just keep calling, and so trainers advise you to say it once, and then if he doesn't come, go to him and physically pull him to the spot from which you called him. The same tactics apply to children, as they, too, learn to tune out. Though I may repeat myself if the child is very young or has a harder time with comprehension, in time I'll ask him to do something only once. I may say, "Robbie, please go sit on the toilet," and if he doesn't, I'd follow up with "Robbie, I'm going to count to three, and if you're not sitting on the toilet, I'm going to help your body." Then you must follow through; you must lift him and put him on the toilet.

EMMA TIP

Kids do not like to be bored. If your child resists doing a chore such as setting the table, instead of asking her five times (which is already too many!), say, "I need you to set the table. This is the last time I'm asking, and then you're going to be sitting on the floor doing *absolutely nothing* until you find your listening ears." You're not giving them a time-out; you're just giving them a choice between being bored and doing what you've asked them to do. Chances are, they'll choose the latter. But be careful: kids are incredibly smart. A stomachache, a need for a snack, or a "fake" injury may arise. The moment you engage with her about it, she is no longer bored, and you, my friend, have become her entertainment.

☑ **Is your child able to talk to you? Do you hear her, listen to her, and respond?**

It's not acceptable for your child to interrupt you, and you mustn't interrupt her. When your child is talking, act interested, nod your head to show you are listening, and say things like "I see," "Mmm, no kidding!" or "Really? Wow."

Be *available* for your child to talk to you. If you can't give your child attention at the moment she wants it, let her know that you want to hear what she has to say, but it will have to be later. Be specific about when. "I'd love to hear the song you learned today, but I have to go change the laundry first. When I've finished, I'd love for you to sing it for me." Then, once you've done what you needed to do, follow up and ask her to sing you the song.

Part of being available means having times worked into your day that welcome communication, times when your child will be able to count on you being there. Talk during mealtime, bath time, and when you are dressing her. Any time she is reliant on you is a great opportunity to interact. **It is so easy to be only half-present. Don't be.**

Finally, being available means allowing give-and-take in conversations. You want the conversation to flow back and forth, like a Ping-Pong game. It always fascinates me to see how even young babies can—and love—to participate in the back and forth of conversation. They love to coo, and then wait while you coo, and then they coo again. We're hard-wired to want equal exchanges, so make sure you are talking *and* listening!

☑ Are you reading your child's body language?

Parents are extraordinary experts on reading their child's movements, from the eye and ear rubs that indicate she's ready for bed to the jittery leg movement that says your preschooler needs to use the potty. Never stop being a student of your child's body language, no matter the circumstances. If she has less energy than usual and is looking down (or whatever your child's cues are), point it out: "You're looking down a lot and don't seem okay. How are you feeling?" Communication is listening as much as speaking, and you need to listen to verbal and nonverbal cues alike to assess your child's needs.

☑ Do you wait until your child is calm before communicating with her?

If your child is either incredibly hyper or incredibly distressed, she will not hear what it is you have to say—there's nothing more to it. You must wait until she's calmed down. This seems quite obvious, and yet parents are constantly trying to communicate with their crazed beast of a tantruming child, and then they become frustrated when the child doesn't absorb what they're saying. (I would actually argue this is a good thing to remember with adults as well—never

EMMA TIP

Just as body language is an important piece of communication for you when you are "reading" your children, it is also helpful for them to read their own bodies. This skill takes time to develop, but it's never too early to start. "How is your body feeling?" is a simple and great question to encourage children to tune in to what's going on. If you sense they are hungry, you might say, "Does your tummy feel empty?" Or if they seem exhausted, sit with them and encourage them to listen to what their bodies are telling them. "Is your body telling you that you want to lie down for a rest? Let's listen." In time, they will be able to vocalize to you what they're feeling and what they need, without your prompting.

try to make progress with *anyone* when tempers are flaring!) If your child is kicking and screaming because she wanted a cookie and you said no, this is not the time to talk to her. Remove her from danger, encourage her to calm down, and ignore her until she has. Let her know that you're there once she's ready. Then, once the tears are dried and her breathing is back to normal, you can calmly and quietly talk about how her response was not appropriate, why, and what you expect next time.

☑ Are you encouraging your child to use his words instead of whining or crying?

Kids go through a whining phase, and if you respond to the whining, it just encourages it. I'm a huge fan of the phrase "use your words." I'm so famous for saying it that one of my clients even added a verse to the song "Wheels on the Bus" for me: "The Emmas on the bus say 'Use your words, use your words, use your words!'" I took it as a compliment! Whether a child is two or five, say, "I can't understand you when you're whining. Use your words, please," or "I can't understand you, so I can't help you." It's amazing how a child *will* stop and find her words. Whining is a habit that takes a lot of patience and repetition to break, but you *can* break it!

☑ Are the adults in your child's life consistent with one another?

One of the trickiest bits of this area doesn't involve communication with your child at all, but communication with others who also care for your child. Parents, grandparents, stepparents, nannies, and teachers may all have responsibility for your child at different points in a day or week, and it's so, so important that everyone be on the same page, or close to it. If parents, in particular, are not on the same page as each other, then even if one parent is doing everything perfectly, it's likely all for nothing. One parent may enforce boundaries and calmly discipline when necessary, but the other parent may be relaxed and refuse to correct the child when he acts out. It's not fair to the parent enforcing the boundaries, and it's not fair to the child. The child isn't receiving a clear message, and his behavior will reflect that.

Communicate often, and formally, with your partner. Sit down together and discuss what rules are important to you, and what your expectations are. Ask, "What exactly do we want from our kids, and how are we going to get it?" Parents have very different ideas sometimes about what should or shouldn't be allowed, and you must come to a meeting of the minds without the kids present so that you are able to convey a united front. To this end, never disempower your spouse in front of the children (unless of course there's some sort of abuse going on, in which case it should go without saying that all bets are off). But if Mum says, "There's no TV tonight," Dad mustn't say, "Why not?" He might pull mum aside and ask her, but not in front of the children, which would undermine her, taking away all her power. And the same goes for Mum. If Dad is letting the kids have huge bowls of ice cream and it's nearly bedtime, don't step in and chastise him about doing so. Pull him aside and discuss it, and perhaps next time he'll exercise greater portion control and give them dessert a bit earlier.

From as young as two years old, children learn that if they don't like the answer they get from one parent, they should try the other. For this reason, if there are to be no more sweets that day, for instance, both parents must know. But in busy households, sometimes this information gets lost, particularly during "hand-offs." I recommend having a whiteboard or notebook where caregivers and parents can communicate with each other. Right after little Suzie has lost her stuffed Elmo for the day because she threw it at her sister, write it on the board or in the book. When the next person comes in to look after the children, even if you've forgotten to update them in all the hullabaloo, the day's information is in the notebook. Or if Suzie has had an upset tummy, that ought to be written down as well, so it's known she shouldn't have milk or anything likely to aggravate her sensitive stomach that day. I know these basics seem, well, *basic*, but once you really start paying attention to communication gaps, the more of them you see.

EMMA TIP

Give grandparents latitude, as it's their job to spoil their grandkids a little bit. If children are being spoiled by their grandparents once every week or so, it's fine. But in situations where the grandparents play a greater role, seeing the grandkids daily or even living with them, then they must coordinate with the parents much more thoughtfully. Also, there are some rules that should never be permitted to be broken. Expectations surrounding respect and manners ought never be relaxed, even for a moment. So while at Grandma's house your child might get dessert even if he hasn't eaten all his dinner, he is still expected to use important manners, like saying "please" and "thank you."

PARENT TIP

Try having regular family meetings. We started having these with our four-year-old, and she loves them. We usually start with a short game of some sort, and then we get out a piece of paper to keep track of what we want to talk about. We go around and say one thing we'd like to happen differently, and one thing we think is working really well. My daughter has said, "I don't like that we have chicken all the time for dinner," and we agreed we'd change up the menu. Then I got to say, "I'd like there to be less whining. What do we think we can do about that?" It's gotten to the point where she will even call a family meeting if we haven't had one in a while. I think it gives her a sense of control about what's happening at home, and it's a great way to talk to her about problem behavior at a time when she's really open to hearing it.

Parents who are separated or divorced have particular challenges. Sometimes they don't want to speak to each other at all. Sometimes they don't want to find agreement with the other for a slew of reasons that really have nothing to do with the child. Sometimes a parent wants the child to favor him or her over the other parent. For all the myriad, emotional, complicated reasons behind these challenges, the underlying rule is straightforward: **You must put everything else aside and put your kids first**. I know this is incredibly tricky to do. It's so tricky that in some places, divorces come along with mandated coparenting classes. The not-so-subtle message behind these classes is, "You're likely not in your right mind when it comes to your former spouse, and it will affect your parenting if you're not prepared." My view boils down to this: There is no excuse, none, for putting your child in the middle of whatever is going on with you and the child's other parent. If you are not thinking about the child's best interest, then you are being selfish. I have no tolerance for it, and whether you are my good friend or a perfect stranger, I'm happy to share that opinion vocally. Nothing makes me more furious.

Communication Investigation

If this material has felt like a lot to absorb, fear not. Since every interaction you have with your child is informed by your communication style—whether you're explaining it's bedtime, setting a limit, or sitting down for dinner—you'll see echoes of what I've covered in this chapter throughout the book. But I also encourage you to return to this chapter once more after you've finished the book. How much of your new communication style has become second nature? What do you still need to work on? Where have you noticed the greatest improvements in your home environment? Are there particular areas—be it bedtime, respect, or scheduling—that are particularly fraught with communication breakdowns? The more you can be a detective, an investigator of your communication holes, the sooner you can get on with patching them.

CHAPTER THREE

Soldiering Forth to the Land of Nod

Sleep Secrets

"A good laugh and a long sleep are the best cures in the doctor's book."

—Irish proverb

CHECKLIST #1: THE EASY BITS—DIAGNOSING THE PROBLEM AND SETTING THE SCENE

☑ Is your child behaving well?

☑ Is your child getting enough sleep?

☑ Is your child sleeping in his own bed?

☑ Does your child have a suitable sleep environment?

☑ Are you avoiding high-energy activities before sleep?

☑ Are you giving your child cues for sleep? Are you watching for his?

☑ For babies: Is your baby on a schedule?

☑ For kids: Is your child on a schedule?

☑ Is your child getting enough exercise and fresh air during the day?

☑ Is your child napping regularly?

CHECKLIST #2: THE HARDER BITS—HABITS AND EXPECTATIONS

☑ Can your child put herself to sleep? Are you avoiding "crutches"?

☑ Can you put your child down during the day?

☑ Can your child get back into his bed on his own once he gets out?

☑ Does your child accept when it's bedtime?

☑ Is your child waking up in a decent mood?

☑ Can you rule out nightmares?

CHECKLIST #3: THE *REALLY* HARD BITS—WHEN THE PROBLEM IS YOU

☑ Do you allow your child to cry?

☑ Have you made your expectations clear?

☑ Do you enforce rules around sleep?

☑ Are you consistent?

☑ Are you tuned in?

☑ Are you ready?

STAND BACK, LADIES and gentlemen, as I am now about to enter the fray. Naturally, I am referring to the very fraught issue that is your child's sleep. If you questioned my assertion in the Introduction that parenting has become a free-for-all for judgment, please look no further than the contentious issue of sleep. Parents, grandparents, pediatricians, aunts, friends, and even strangers all have opinions about what it is that will help a child sleep, and they are more than willing to share their guidance and to judge you if you choose not to follow it.

So I am asking you to please leave your judgment at the door for the duration of this chapter, as well as any time you discuss sleep with other parents. When you're tired, a disapproving eye is the last thing any well-meaning parent needs. We're all trying to do right by our kids, so let's start with that baseline and go from there. I promise I'm not going to give you a wallop if you don't follow my advice. I just ask that you read with an open mind.

Let's begin by covering the simple facts I'm sure everyone can agree on:

1. Sleep is critical for your child. In fact, that's why I placed this chapter so early in the book. Of all of the behavioral problems I see, sleep is at the root of perhaps 75 percent of them. While some of the chapters in this book overlap in theme with just one or two others, sleep is connected to positively every other chapter in this book. Even one extra

hour of sleep a day will improve a child's behavior. For older kids, an extra hour of sleep a night improved their grades in school.*

2. Sleep is critical for you. You cannot be at your best if you are not well rested. And you cannot be well rested if your child is up all night. I've worked with many parents who are exhausted after the first six months of their child's life. One father routinely fell asleep at his desk at work. How can you possibly be a good parent when you are that tired?

3. I have more than a dozen years of experience getting children to sleep, and I have learned a few things along the way. Argue with the philosophies of this chapter if you will, but know that the lessons are borne from countless nights spent teaching children to sleep.

Those are the facts.

Now, as for one of my more controversial beliefs, based on what I have learned over the years: As I've said, we've gotten to a place culturally where we are too averse to letting our children experience discomfort. We do not want our children to cry, ever. But consider this: If we don't let them cry, how will we *learn* their cry? You must be a student of your baby, toddler, preschooler, and grade-schooler, a role that is all the more challenging when they are very little and don't have the words to express themselves. So you must listen. You must learn to differentiate the hungry cry from the sleepy cry from the gassy cry. (And by the way, most cries are gassy cries.) You must not be subject to the cultural forces around you, or the high-tech baby monitors that compel you to react to every movement or murmur immediately. Instead, you must stop, listen, and think before you react.

---

* *The Impact of School Start Times on Adolescent Health and Academic Performance* (http://schoolstarttime.org).

Here is the best thing I've learned: your child can and will sleep. Touch wood, every single child I've trained has learned to sleep through the night, and I've trained hundreds of them. Parents frequently tell me, "My child is just not a good sleeper." But I don't believe that. While it's true that some children need less sleep than others, I don't believe in a bad sleeper. Good sleep habits can be taught.

When I do sleep consultations, sometimes I stay with a family for just one night— that's all it takes. Other times I may stay as many as four nights. But in four nights, it's all done and dusted, and the rewards are incredible. There's nothing I love more than when a family that was at the end of their tether begins to get ten hours of sleep a night. They become quite jubilant, really. It's extraordinary and very rewarding.

Sleep is an important issue throughout your little one's childhood. However, it is the greatest source of conversation and consternation for parents of infants. While many of these checklist items will speak to those new, exhausted parents, there are also important boxes to check off for older kids as well, so please have a look.

☑ Is your child behaving well?

Sometimes I'm not called in for a sleep consult at all, but rather a "help me with my out-of-control child!" consult. I observe the child for a bit, and if he's behaving completely irrationally, I usually point the finger at tiredness (or diet, which I cover in the next chapter). Of course there are many reasons for a child to behave irrationally— they are children, after all, and they have their moments! They also have teething problems and upset tummies and all sorts of things that can make them crabby. But as it is for adults, sleep is the key. Most adults, fortunately, are able to say, "I'm crying over spilt milk! Clearly I'm feeling tired and should go to bed early." A two-year-old or five-year-old, however, won't understand why he's feeling the way he's feeling. He just knows that he's frustrated, and we see that he's having tantrums over everything. Or the child may need more sleep, and the parent doesn't even realize it. Which leads to the next question:

☑ Is your child getting enough sleep?

This is quite obviously the first question I ask parents, and the first question parents should ask if their child is acting out. While we must allow for some variation, I have found the following sleep chart—from Children's Hospital at Stanford University*—to be the most useful.

Age	Total sleep hours	Nighttime sleep	Daytime sleep
Newborn	16	8 to 9	8
1 month	15.5	8 to 9	7
3 months	15	9 to 10	4 to 5
6 months	14	10	4
9 months	14	11	3
1 year	14	11	3
1.5 years	13.5 hours	11	2.5
2 years	13	11	2

Once a child is three, I recommend eleven hours of sleep per night, with an afternoon nap or rest time. For four-year-olds and older, ten or more hours of sleep at night is ideal. If your child is getting roughly the amount of sleep required for his age group, lovely. You can move on to some other questions about the quality of that sleep. But if not, you have a starting point and a goal to reach.

* http://www.lpch.org/DiseaseHealthInfo/HealthLibrary/growth/infhab.html.

☑ Is your child sleeping in his own bed?

I once interviewed for a nanny position where my prospective employer wondered if I'd judge her for wanting what's known as a "family bed," where Mum and Dad and brothers and sisters all sleep in the same (hopefully large) bed. My answer is no, of course not—but that doesn't mean I think it's a sensible route to a good night's sleep. I often have cosleeping parents say to me, "Emma, I'm exhausted. The baby's not sleeping and is feeding throughout the night." I tell them what I think they should do, which starts with moving the baby out of their bed. "No," they say, "I can't do that." To which I say, "That's fine, but then I can't help you. When you're ready to move the baby, let me know."

The problem is that in a family bed, the quality of sleep—and also life!—suffers. Even if you choose to cosleep in the early weeks, the moment someone's not getting quality sleep, or your relationship with your partner suffers, or you have to go to bed at eight so your child will, or you have to pass on a fun night out because your child can't sleep without you, there is a problem. It's time to change the sleep arrangement. I could go on for pages with stories of families I've worked with who have had just this problem. The family bed worked well for them in the beginning, but then when it stopped working, they didn't know how to break the habit, or they weren't willing to. A large part of the problem is parents don't believe their children can sleep without them. Erase that thought. They can, and thinking they won't only defeats you at the outset. If you do everything on this checklist, they will sleep. Repeat that as many times as you must, and move the little one out of your bed.

One family I worked with had two-year-old triplets, and the parents and all three little boys slept on a mattress on the floor in the parents' bedroom. For anyone who's ever had trouble falling asleep when your partner is tossing and turning, imagine *five bodies* all trying to settle down at once. It's simply asking for trouble. One finally settles down as another gets wound up, then perhaps everyone settles down but the one in the middle has to go to the loo. It's like playing the arcade game Whack-a-Mole, and who needs to do that when you just want to go to sleep? In the case of the triplets, it was apparent the children were exhausted, and so were the parents. It was time for the boys to have their own beds.

I also see many kids sleeping in a car seat or in their stroller. "It's the only way I can get him to sleep!" say the parents. The parents are so desperate, they drive their children around in the car, then let them sleep in their car seats until they wake up. Or they put them in their strollers and walk them around the block to get them to sleep. I've known parents who swore the only way they could get their three-year-old to sleep was to walk her around the neighborhood in the Ergo (a popular baby carrier), and I've known mums who refuse to move after their baby has fallen asleep on their boob. No, no, no! Babies should sleep in their cribs, and children should sleep in their beds. It might not be the most pleasant experience to teach them how, but you can teach them, they will do it, and everyone will be happier and better rested for it.

> EMMA TIP
>
> Children need to realize they are independent beings, that they are separate from their parents. It helps them operate in the world much better. The more they grow accustomed to sleeping on their own, the more they feel confident operating in other ways on their own. A five-year-old who still sleeps in his parents' bed is likely to panic when invited to a friend's house for a sleepover, so start teaching him the skills early on that he will need to go into the world on his own.

☑ Does your child have a suitable sleep environment?

You'd be shocked by the extent of goodies in some children's beds. One boy I worked with insisted on sleeping with sticks. Sticks! That's all well and good for camping, perhaps, but is hardly safe and comfortable for a good night's sleep. A bed filled with toys, books, and cuddly animals is too stimulating. For that matter, so is a room overflowing with toys, such that it looks more like a playground than a place of rest. Be moderate in the amount of toys you have at one time and in one room, and if possible, have a toy chest, closet, wicker basket, or bookshelf where everything can rest out of your child's immediate line of sight for the evening.

I suggest parents let their child choose one special thing for their bed—be it their lovie or their special bear. (No sticks, though, *please*!) I make sure that the room is at a reasonable temperature, such as the high sixties. I make sure that what they're sleeping in is breathable, like cotton, and soft. I sometimes see kids go to sleep with all these snaps and buttons down their backs. When you put them down on their back, all they're sleeping on is metal, all the way down their spine! Comfort is much more important than style or anything else, even if your sweet Aunt Hildy meant well when she sent you those jammies.

I like a dark, quiet room and am not a big advocate of sound machines. However, you must have realistic expectations. If some-

EMMA TIP

Lovies, by which I mean security blankets, can be great for sleep, but they need to stay in the bed. Don't let your child take it in the car or stroller, or even to the kitchen table. Not only might it get lost, but your child needs to learn to cope without it. It's good for her self-esteem to limit her dependence on an object like a lovie. Also, the lovie should be associated only with sleep.

one's hammering or having a party next door, or if your baby is a consistently light sleeper, then use a sound machine, by all means. But at the same time, don't be a hostage to noise. If you need to run the vacuum cleaner while the baby's sleeping, for instance, do it. By making some noise, you might just inure her to it. And she will be grateful when she reaches college and must get a good night's sleep while a progressive party is happening in her dormitory.

☑ Are you avoiding high-energy activities before sleep?

It seems obvious, right? It's not sensible to engage in activities that will get your children wound up before bedtime. We all need time to settle down and for our energy levels to slow a bit. And yet this is often very challenging for parents. For one, the *parents* aren't tired—it may be only seven thirty, so Mum and Dad are prepared to be up for another several hours. They may have a hard time matching the calm, slow energy their children need. Also, many parents don't get home from work until close to bedtime, and they want to play with their children. One father I know loved to "ruckus" with his kids, which amounted to wrestling on the bed. The children only saw him for an hour or so in the evenings, and this was a special part of their time together. The dad was loath to let it go—he loved and needed it at the end of his day, just as his kids looked forward to it. But the pre-bedtime ruckus made it much harder for the children to settle down. Ultimately he compromised and ruckused with them only on nights when he was home early enough to still allow for wind-down time, and he implemented what he called "shorthand ruckus" where he would do one or two fun physical things with the kids and then it was time to calm down.

While the "ruckus" is an obvious example of energizing children, a less obvious one is television. One family I worked with allowed the children to watch television in bed at night in order to settle down. Our first order of business was removing the TVs from the kids' bedrooms; children's brains (and adults' for that matter) can't wind down and go to sleep well after the stimulation the screen offers.

Another less apparent source of energy is a glass of milk. Typically I avoid giving children milk before naptime, but milk is an example where you really need to tune into your child and see what affect it's having. Some children are not affected at all by milk, and some children will go to sleep right after the milk but then they'll wake up thirty minutes later, buzzing with energy. To be safe, I will give a child milk perhaps forty minutes or so before his nap, to make sure he's full but not overly stimulated by having a full tummy. For young babies, I feed them upon wake-up.

☑ Are you giving your child cues for sleep? Are you watching for his?

It's important for all of us to have a bit of a transition between playtime and sleep time, and this is where the sleep cue comes in (which is far, far different from a sleep crutch). For babies, the cues might be swaddling and a little rocking. (I am a strong supporter of swaddling, incidentally. Until they are big and strong enough to break out of the swaddle, it can be a great cue for a baby's sleep, and is incredibly comforting.) For older kids, it might be getting into their PJs and reading a special sleep-time book or listening to a calming lullaby. Also watch for *their* cues. Eye rubbing, yawning, and fussiness are the most common cues children give when they're tired, but every child is different, so take care to learn *your* child's cues.

☑ For babies: Is your baby on a schedule?

Healthy sleep habits start early. While you should certainly do whatever you must to muddle through in an infant's early weeks, you can start differentiating day from night almost immediately with your baby. It can be as simple as putting her in her swaddle and dimming the lights or singing a soothing song while you rock her.

As long as your newborn is gaining weight appropriately in the first week or two, you can also begin to put her on a feeding schedule. I encourage you to check in with your pediatrician to make sure weight gain is not an issue, and then you ought to resist feeding on demand. A healthy infant should eat only every 2.5 or 3 hours. (See Chapter Four for more on this!)

Schedules make life easier. When my friend Silvia, who is also a trained nanny, just had her first baby, Silvia's mum came and stayed to help out for the first few months. Everything went seamlessly. Silvia's mum was always available to hold the baby. The baby slept with Silvia at night and took periodic catnaps during the day. But when Mum left, Silvia was a mess. She couldn't get anything done with her now four-month-old. She was always holding her and felt like a slave to the baby's uncertain naptime routine. She asked for my help, and I suggested she get on a schedule. Silvia eased into the schedule slowly. First she established feed times, then naptimes, then a consistent bedtime. The baby started sleeping through the night. It sounds simple, but sometimes simple works. It worked for Silvia and it will work for you. When babies have a schedule, sleep is easier.

When a baby is eight to ten weeks old, so long as you have your doctor's approval, it's time to start pushing the night feedings further apart. You might feed your baby at 7:00 p.m. and then 10:30, but then you will want to push the next feeding to four hours away, then five, then eventually six! The less dependent she becomes on the nighttime feedings, the sooner you will break the habit of her wanting calories at night.

If your baby is older than five months and you are still feeding him through the night, unless your pediatrician has told you to because the baby has a medical condition, you should stop. By the time babies are five or six months old, they do not need to be eating during the night at all and should be sleeping through for at least ten hours. If she wakes up in the interim, respond, but not immediately. Do what you must to calm her down without feeding her. For those of you who are thinking, *Emma, that sounds lovely, but how in heaven's name am I supposed to do that?* don't worry. Read on. But first, here are some sample schedules that might prove helpful:

SIX MONTHS

Time awake	6:00 to 7:00 a.m.
Breakfast (milk and solids)	Milk upon wakening; solids at 7 a.m.
Playtime	8:00 to 9:30 a.m.
Sleep time	9:30/10:00 a.m. (at least 1 1/2 to 2 hours)
Lunch (milk and solids)	Milk upon wakening; solids at noon
Playtime	12:30 to 2:00 p.m.
Sleep time	2:00 to 4:00 p.m. (needs to be 1 to 2 hours)
Feed time	Milk upon wakening
Playtime	Until 5:00 or 5:30 p.m.
Solids	5:00 or 5:30 p.m.
Playtime	5:45 to 6:45 pm
Bath time	6:45 p.m.
Bedtime/last feed	7:00 p.m.

17 MONTHS

Time awake	6:00 to7:00 a.m.
Breakfast	6:00 to 7:00 a.m.
Playtime	8:00 to 10:00 a.m.
Sleep time	10:00 to 11:30 a.m. (should be between 1 and 2 hours)
Lunch	12:00 p.m.
Playtime	1:00 to 2:30 p.m.
Sleep time	2:30 to 4:00 p.m. (around 1 hour)
Dinner	5:00 p.m.
Playtime and bath	5:45 to 6:30 or 7:00 p.m.
Bedtime/last feed (milk, and don't forget to brush teeth!)	7:00 to 7:30 p.m.

Please note, these schedules are guidelines and should not be followed rigidly.

☑ For kids: Is your child on a schedule?

Before I come to stay in a family's home for a sleep consult, I ask about the child's routine, and often I ask the family to overhaul it *before* I come—or to create a schedule if they don't have one. Many families I work with will have breakfast at 6:00 a.m. some days, 7:00 a.m. on others, and sometimes not until 8:00 a.m. That's unacceptable, as *mealtimes keep time to the rhythms of a child's day and night.* I want to be sure they're eating at consistent times throughout the day. Breakfast ought to always be at roughly the same time. Bedtime, likewise, must be at the same time, and there must be a set bedtime routine.

You want bedtime to be consistent, give or take fifteen minutes.

You don't want to miss the all-important window between when a child is tired and when he is overtired. If you keep him up because Daddy is almost home and wants to see him before bedtime, he is apt to get overtired and then, ironically, more energized. The proverbial second wind begins once the bedtime window has shut, and it's not a wind that is welcome, for meltdowns are not far behind. As I've already made clear, parents get into trouble when they are too attentive to their child's every need. But there is a balance, and sleep is an excellent example of where Mum and Dad need to put aside their own needs. With a few exceptions, your child needs a consistent schedule. If a parent wants to see him before he goes off to the land of nod, then the parents must get home before the child's bedtime or just resolve to see him in the morning.

☑ Is your child getting enough exercise and fresh air during the day?

There's nothing quite like fresh air and exercise to ensure a good night's sleep. If a child is overly sedentary, his sleep will suffer. If a child never gets outside to play and blow off energy, his sleep will suffer. I look for outside activities in a child's schedule, and if they are not a regular part of his day, I ask that they be incorporated before nighttime is even dealt with at all.

☑ Is your child napping regularly?

Sleep begets sleep. The more sleep he's getting, the more he will sleep. If a child skips his nap, he is apt to become overtired. And he's likely to be a monster at different moments in the day, making neither parent terribly happy. The question of whether naps are his problem is easy enough to answer. Solving it is an entirely different matter altogether, and I'll get into that soon enough.

☑ Can your child put herself to sleep? Are you avoiding "crutches"?

How do you get your child to sleep? Do you

a. rock her until she's sound asleep, then transfer her to her bed or crib;

b. put her in her crib or bed and allow her to put herself to sleep; or

c. walk her or drive her around until she's asleep, and then leave her wherever she's fallen asleep?

You probably know the correct answer is b, but that doesn't mean you do it. I'm here to remind you that crutches, or shortcuts, create longer roads. *Resist the easy path to the short-term payoff and take the long view.* This means putting children—even infants—down awake so that they learn how to fall asleep. You are likely familiar with the phrase "Give a man a fish and feed him today. Teach a man to fish and feed him forever." This means you cannot breastfeed your baby to sleep and then put him down ever so softly. You cannot rock him to sleep. You cannot sing him to sleep. You cannot lie in bed with him until he's asleep. After he's about three months old, you cannot give him a pacifier to help him go to sleep. These are all shortcuts, and they are all equivalent to giving a man a fish. When the pacifier falls out, the child will need it to go back to sleep. When he wakes up (as all of us do, in subtle ways, throughout the night), he will need whatever that crutch was to get him to sleep again and again. In most cases, this means he will need *you*.

Take the time to teach your baby or child to fall asleep himself, and while you will have a few difficult days, you will make your life so much easier. Eliminate crutches, and your child will learn how to self-soothe, and get to sleep on his own.

> EMMA TIP
>
> Never let children have milk in the crib. It's dangerous, it's bad for the teeth, it's messy, and it creates a bad habit. Perhaps it's easier in the short-term to put your child down with milk, but definitely not in the long-term, so resist!

☑ *Can you put your child down during the day?*

Parents so often feel like they have to hold or engage their child all day long. I've heard parent after parent say, "She's just sitting there on her mat. I should probably be talking to her or reading to her or something, right?" They feel liberated when I say, "No, not at all." The more you can put down your baby, letting her play on the floor, the better. It's unreasonable to expect a baby will go to sleep on her own at night if she's been touched and held and entertained the entire day.

That's not to say that I'm against baby carriers—they can be wonderful and practical, and I especially utilize them when a baby is gassy or fussy. If your baby needs closeness, don't deprive her of it. But if she's been cuddled and she's happy, take that opportunity to pop her on the floor and let her play. You can hold her as much as you like, but you also must be able to put her down or you won't be able to accomplish anything—this is as much for your own sanity as anything else, trust me! At the very least, you need to be able to put her in a car seat if you need to go anywhere. You simply must teach her that sometimes, she must amuse herself. It will make sleep much easier, because it's a lesson she'll have already learned.

☑ Can your child get back into his bed on his own once he gets out?

If an older child (by which I mean one who is not in a crib) is frequently getting out of bed, there is usually a reason he's doing so. And it's usually to get attention (i.e., you putting him back in). That is why once a child is physically able to climb out of his bed, he also needs to be able to get back in by himself. If he climbs out and wants you to put him back in, you can do so a few times, but then make it clear that if he gets out again, he needs to get back in himself. He may protest by sleeping on the floor—which is fine—but he will probably realize his bed is more comfortable and will climb back in himself. The key is that he not be reliant on you to put him back. Children more often than not will use whatever they can to manipulate a situation, and I mean that in the most complimentary way—they are little geniuses! Whether it's "just one more book," rocking to sleep, or simply needing you to put them back to bed . . . eliminate it all. Make them responsible. Say, "I'll tuck you in and make you cozy, but this is the last time I'm doing it. You need to stay in bed. If you get out again you'll have to tuck yourself in."

☑ Does your child accept when it's bedtime?

A whole category of books has been written about children resisting bedtime. Mo Willems's *Don't Let the Pigeon Stay Up Late* comes to mind, as does Adam Mansbach's humor book for grown-ups, *Go the F**k to Sleep*. So know that if your child resists bedtime, it may be just part of childhood and not because of anything you're doing wrong. In fact, some kids will always cry when they go to bed, although usually it's just for a minute. That's how they soothe themselves, and how they go to sleep. Be prepared to let *them* let down their remaining resistance to bedtime.

☑ Is your child waking up in a decent mood?

If your child is clearly waking up too early—meaning that he should be getting eleven hours of sleep but is getting only nine, or he takes a thirty-minute nap and that's it—wait a few minutes to see if he'll go back to sleep on his own, then go into his room and tell him it's still time for sleep. Avoid picking him up. If he continues to cry, I would go back in after a bit, and explain once more he needs to lie there until it's time to get up. If your child continues the early waking the next day or two, continue going in as explained above and let him know it's still time for sleep.

If you think a child is waking up too early because he wakes up cranky—either from a nap or from nighttime sleep—then pay close attention. Just as some children always cry in order to go to sleep, some children always cry when they wake up. It's part of their transition. If this is the case, don't go to them right away—give them time to wake up. Perhaps they'll go back to sleep, or perhaps they'll lie there grumpy for a bit until they can snap out of it. They're not unlike adults, really. We all like to hit the snooze button on occasion in order to transition ourselves into our day. And children don't even have the benefit of coffee to aid them with facing their morning!

However, sometimes children really do wake up earlier than they should, and their fussiness is different from what I refer to as "transition fussiness." One little guy I took care of would always be grumpy when he woke up from his nap, but if it took more than ten minutes or so for him to snap out of it, I would say, "Daren, I think you've gotten up on the wrong side of the bed. You need to go back to sleep." And I would ask him to rest his body for a bit.

☑ Can you rule out nightmares?

I take nightmares quite seriously. When a four-year-old comes to your room frightened in the middle of the night, you must acknowledge that fear. Ask her about her dream. If she is afraid of monsters in the closet or under the bed, turn on the light and do what you must to show her that her bedroom is safe. Nighttime anxiety can be ongoing and very tricky to master for a little brain and body, so help her manage it in whatever way you can. Explain that whatever she dreamed is not real. Even pull her into bed with you if she's truly frightened. It may surprise you that I'm actually not such a stickler for never allowing your child into your bed. The important thing is that it not become a habit. If she crawls into your bed claiming nightmares night after night, then what began as a single bad dream has become a perpetual bad habit. You must be very attentive to whether your child is truly scared, or just pulling the wool over your eyes. Chances are good that you will be able to distinguish between the two.

> EMMA TIP
>
> If nightmares are a recurrent problem, pay closer attention to what your child is watching or reading. Many books and television shows that on the surface seem harmless are actually frightening to children.

☑ Do you allow your child to cry?

Imagine you have put your child down for a nap. While usually she will nap for at least an hour, today you hear her wake up after thirty minutes. Do you

a. ignore it—you are off-duty for another thirty minutes, and she will just have to stay in her crib;

b. go to her quickly;

c. let her fuss for a few minutes and listen to the cry? Does she put herself back to sleep? Is she tired? Might she have had a poop that's startled her out of her sleep?

The correct answer is c, but I know that's not the answer parents usually want. They don't want their child to cry, *ever*. To which I say, where is the balanced-parenting approach in that?

Once I've looked at everything that could possibly be getting in the way of a child's sleep—from his routine to his bed to his pajamas—and it all looks good, then nine times out of ten, the parent is the problem. The parent is either relying on some kind of crutch to help the child sleep—such as nursing or a pacifier or a bottle in the crib—or she is going immediately to her child's aid, not giving him enough time to help himself.

I do not think parents should ignore their children, as in answer a (some nanny I would be if I did suggest such a thing!), but it's a far distance between abandonment and allowing a child to cry long enough so that you can learn the cry. You need to be able to identify whether the cry is signaling pain or just the tiredness that comes right before sleep. I know it's hard, but *you will never learn her cry unless you* ***let*** *her cry*. Before you react to your baby's cry, stop and think, *Did I feed her?* If you did, then you know she's not hungry—and the more you have her on an eating schedule, the easier it will be to determine. If it's bedtime, and she's woken up just thirty minutes after going down, ask yourself, *Is she tired? Did she nap well?* That could well be the problem—if she didn't nap well, she may be crying simply because she's tired and you need to let her let it out. *Could she be in pain?* With newborns, gas is incredibly common, and I believe in comforting a gassy baby. The more you learn the cry, the more you will learn if the problem is gas. If it is, then by all means lift her and comfort her. (But don't feed her! See page 92.) Though this may seem vague, there really is a certainty and a magic that comes when you listen to your child and trust what you hear.

Here's a quick chart of the most common sleep-time cries and how I handle them:

Whining, tired cry: Leave her be. She just needs to get it out of her system and put herself to sleep.

Hysterical cry: Go to her, especially if she's younger. She needs calming. Pat her back, sing to her, calm her down before leaving again.

Sad cry: She needs reassurance. Go in and give her that reassurance, gently reminding her that it's time to sleep before you leave.

Another absolute certainty is that you simply cannot go in after a child's been crying for just a minute. It's not long enough to learn the cry, though I know it can feel like forever. In general I am not fond of timers dictating when you go in to check on your child—there's no set formula when you're really listening to your child, and the child doesn't know the difference between five minutes and ten minutes—but I do think timers can be helpful for *parents*. When that minute feels like forever, the timer can help remind you that no, it's hasn't been long and you need to give your child time to settle himself down.

Prepare yourself that you might have some difficult nights before it gets better. But it will get better, and you will all sleep.

A WORD ON NAPS

The time and place for naps should be as consistent as possible. I know that sometimes it's difficult to structure your entire day around a nap that might or might not happen, and I am not always rigid about nap schedules. But if your child is not sleeping well or regularly at night or during the day, then move heaven and earth to keep his sleeping schedule the same for at least three days. If it goes well and then you need to make a change or run out on an errand during naptime, so be it.

Once a child drops her nap, I am a firm believer in rest time. Everyone needs some time to rest their bodies, relax, switch off, and not engage for a while—including Mum and Dad! Don't despair if your child has given up her nap while you savored that time for yourself. Set her up with books she can look at quietly in her room for the same period each and every day, and tell her she needs to rest her body. It may be a struggle at first, but one that will be well worth it and improve both of your behavior!

☑ **Have you made your expectations clear?**

Parents are constantly befuddled that their child sleeps perfectly at daycare—two hours each day, without a fuss—even amid a dozen other sleeping little bodies. How do the teachers do it? The answer is simple: they set the expectation. A daycare teacher cannot have children sleeping at different times, for it would be chaos. Naptime is non-negotiable. The teachers make their expectations clear, and the children nine times out

PARENT TIP

My husband and I have found it helpful to plan our nighttime approach ahead of time. The key is getting clarity right up front about what we'll do if our son wakes up. Negotiating a sleep philosophy at 2:00 a.m. is not good!

of ten adhere to them. (And if the tenth child doesn't sleep, she knows she must be quiet.) Parents can learn a thing or two from daycares on this point. Parents must be very clear about what bedtime will look like, even with very young children. They might say, "I'm going to read you two books, and then I'm going to turn out the light. If you come out of your room after that, I'm going to put you back in. If you wake up in the middle of the night, you'll need to go back to sleep."

☑ Do you enforce rules around sleep?

Once you've been clear about your expectations, stick with them. If you've said you'll read two books, read two books. The moment you start reading three or four, the moment you're talked into letting your child get another cup of water, or allowing another minute of snuggling after you've said you're leaving, you've lost control. Be strong and resolved, and do what you tell your child you're going to do. Do the same thing night after night, and make sure whoever puts your child down for bed is doing the same thing.

☑ Are you consistent?

Consistency is everything, and I won't apologize for saying so again and again. (That's being consistent, after all!) The worst thing is to allow your child to cry one night, but then not the next, and so on. She will receive mixed messages and be very confused. You won't come any closer to fixing the problem, and you'll be a wreck. Save yourself the ordeal. Decide that you will commit to letting your child cry for three nights. Yes, there will be some crying on both your parts, but soon everyone will be sleeping. I take issue with methods that suggest backing away from your child little by little until you're finally out the door. To me, that's a bit like dangling a carrot in front of them, and hardly seems fair.

☑ Are you tuned in?

Learning your child's cry is part of being tuned in, but there are other ways to ensure that you are really paying attention to what's going on with your child. If you've had a particularly busy week at work or have other personal matters going on, and your child isn't sleeping well for reasons you can't determine, take a breath. Slow down. Think about the rhythms of your child's life and moods. If you have a child who sleeps through the night, and then one night he's up crying, you know there's something going on. In such a circumstance, I would not recommend letting him cry for minutes on end. It's time to investigate. If his cheeks are rosy, and his nappies (diapers) are different than usual, he may be teething. Take a look at his gums and teeth and see if a tooth is trying to poke its way through. Or perhaps he's sick. If he needs extra TLC, give it to him. If he needs medicine, give it to him. Give him whatever he needs if he's having a bad night, short of feeding him. When you've established an excellent baseline and your child goes off it, it's very possible something's going on that needs your attention. (There are also occasions when kids fall off their schedules for no apparent reason. Once you've checked for teething and illness and found neither is present, it's possibly just one of these unknown phases you'll have to wait out!)

The problem with changing the ground rules, of course, is that then you will have to reestablish the expectations around sleep once he's well again. You'll need to repeat what you've learned each time something throws a spanner in the works, be it teething or a fever or returning from a vacation. Parents get defeated by how quickly the training goes out the window. But it gets easier each time, I promise. Habits are formed in as little as a day.

☑ Are you ready?

If you have not allowed your child to cry and are going to begin, make sure you're ready. Remember that the hardest scenario is to start and not be able to follow through, because with inconsistency, everything goes out the window. I always tell parents how hard it's going to be. I prepare them as much as I prepare the child, really. It's hard for me to listen to a child cry, too, and I'm not emotionally attached the way the parent is. I know how tough it is, but it helps to remember all of the reasons you're letting the child continue. If a parent feels like she is about to give in, she should look at a list of all of those reasons she is taking this route—reasons she needs to sleep, reasons her baby needs to sleep. Keeping your eye on the ultimate goal is one thing when you're reading these words in the late evening, but another matter entirely when it's 3:00 a.m. and your baby has been crying on and off for what feels like hours.

> **PARENT TIP**
>
> When we were sleep training, I was on the phone with my parents and friends for all of the crying. It kept me from going in to comfort the baby when I wasn't supposed to, and I got pep talks.

It's Okay if You Make Mistakes

When I was fairly new to child care, I fell into my share of sleep traps. I would rock a baby to sleep, set her down ever so gently, then tiptoe out of the room, keeping my fingers crossed that she wouldn't wake up again. It was exhausting and time consuming, and I'd inevitably have to repeat the process a dozen times throughout the night when she couldn't go back to sleep without my help. I've used pacifiers. I've picked up children convinced they had a poo, only to see I'd misread the cry. I've caved to a crying child in the middle of the night, and thus been inconsistent. Happily, now that I have years more of experience and dozens of carefully studied sleep books under my belt, I don't make those mistakes anymore. What's more, I don't really look back on those experiences and worry that the children suffered. They were fine—if anything, I had a much harder go of it than they did! This is all to say that if you've embarked on a different course before reading this chapter, don't feel chastised or alarmed that it's too late. Children learn easily, and you can still help them connect the dots to get a good night's sleep. Bad habits can be broken, and the fact that you let your four-month-old use a pacifier for a time does not a bad parent make. Just toss it out now, please, if you would. And let's get on to a good night's sleep.

CHAPTER FOUR

A Tale of Porridge and Pudding

Proper Nutrition

"... he'll eat when he gets hungry. Why don't you just leave him alone!"

—Nine-year-old Peter Hatcher to his mum, *Tales of a Fourth Grade Nothing*, by Judy Blume

CHECKLIST

☑ Do you back off if your child doesn't want to eat?

☑ Is your child a healthy weight?

☑ Does your child eat at regular intervals? Do you also avoid constant snacking?

☑ Does your child sit down to eat?

☑ Does your child have good table manners?

☑ Do you limit the amount of sugar in your child's diet?

☑ Are you offering a varied diet?

☑ Do you prevent your child from filling up on beverages?

☑ Do you avoid removing "offensive" food from your child's plate?

☑ Is your child aware of what he's eating?

☑ Are you a good role model around food and nutrition?

☑ Do you monitor the quality and quantity of snack food available?

☑ Are your expectations reasonable?

☑ Do you offer incentives like dessert, but not too often?

☑ Do you give your child a choice?

☑ Do you routinely introduce new foods?

☑ Do you persist if your child doesn't like something the first time he tries it?

☑ Do you avoid food games?

☑ Are you trusting your instincts about your child's weight?

When I was growing up in England, mealtimes served an important purpose in our family life. My mum was raising my brother and me on her own for much of that time, and we didn't have a lot of money, but meals—dinner in particular—were still special. We would sit down together over shepherd's pie or bubble and squeak (sautéed potatoes and cabbage—yum!) and discuss our day. We didn't spend hours over the meal, but nor did we rush it. On Sundays my nana would come over as well, and the meal would be more elaborate, with a nice tablecloth, a roast to eat, and usually a spotted dick (a cake with dried fruit) or apple crumble for pudding (by which I mean dessert). Our meals weren't fancy, and they do not qualify as one of my favorite memories of childhood. But there was something so *essential* about them. They laid a baseline for my relationship with food throughout my life. They gave me a sense of grounding and of ritual. There was a great deal of comfort in knowing that they would happen each day regardless of whatever else was going on in my life.

I was surprised when I moved to the United States and saw how differently meals were handled, by families and nannies alike. Most of my American nanny friends fed their charges on the run: in the car, in a stroller, or running around the kitchen. The food was typically whatever the child asked for, or whatever was a safe bet (like macaroni and cheese or fried chicken strips). Most foods were finger foods, and children weren't encouraged or taught how to use utensils. It bothered me, and I began to wonder why I cared. Why did eating the way I was taught matter so much? And why was it so different in America?

I've given these questions a lot of thought over the years, and I believe a large part of the problem is the changing role of food. In our runaround lives full of too many activities, food has taken a supporting role when it should have a starring one. It's not revelatory that eating meals together is important, and yet contemporary culture devalues not only the ritual but also the food itself. Food is consumed, not savored. Mealtimes are seen as serving the goal of "refueling," rather than opportunities to connect and teach things like appreciation for flavor and proper table manners.

The other part of the problem is that as with so much else, parents cater too much to their children when it comes to food. I recently read in a parenting book that if a child doesn't want to eat what you're eating, that you should allow him to get up from the table and make himself a sandwich or some other simple meal. *Unbelievable!* I couldn't disagree more. This sends the message that he does not need to eat what is put in front of him, and guess what? While he has the option of making something else to eat, he *won't* eat what's in front of him. It also sends the message that it's okay to be moving about while everyone else is eating. And you will likely end up with twice the amount of mess to clean up. Sometimes Mum or Dad will make special meals for their child in order to get her to eat, or go even further. In Judy Blume's classic book *Tales of a Fourth Grade Nothing*, when three-year-old Fudge refuses to eat, the family goes through incredible antics to entice him. Fudge's brother Peter stands on his head so that Fudge will laugh and his mum can get a bite of food in his mouth. Fudge's grandmother makes milkshakes with egg inside. Fudge's mother allows him to sit underneath the table and pretend he's the family dog, so long as he'll eat that way. While these may seem a bit extreme, they're funny precisely because they're familiar.

I have two pieces of good news in this chapter. The first is that you do not have to cater to your children and be an on-demand cook. Your family kitchen is not a restaurant, so don't let your children treat it like one! The second is that mealtime does not have to represent a battleground, or a circus, like in the case of Fudge. And the simple solution that makes all of this possible is that *parents need to be okay with letting their children go hungry sometimes.* From the time your child is roughly twelve months old and not dependent on milk as her main source of nutrition, you can expect the same of her that you would expect of an older child. If your child doesn't want to eat, you can't force her. There's no fight; she doesn't have to eat. But you shouldn't give her anything else, either. Give her a chance, explain there is nothing else until the next mealtime (even if that's breakfast the next day), and it's her choice if she doesn't want to eat. This rule applies to older children, too—there's no difference between young ones and older ones on this point. Then she should still sit at the table until everyone else is finished. **But the prolonged negotiations, fights, coaxing, and plain energy devoted to getting a child to eat are gone. Kids will eat when they're hungry.** All you have to do is provide nutritional food, occasionally put food on the table that you know they'll like, and take the pressure off the entire situation. If you haven't been following this philosophy all along, don't worry—it won't take long at all before your children understand that the restaurant has closed for business, so to speak, and there's a new set of expectations. *Finit!*

☑ *Do you back off if your child doesn't want to eat?*

If your child doesn't want to eat what you've served, do you

a. tell him that what's in front of him is what's for dinner, and if he doesn't want it, he doesn't have to eat it;

b. make him something else;

c. coax him to eat, bite by bite, by game-playing and offering rewards with each mouthful;

d. threaten to take away privileges (such as television or a nighttime book)?

As you probably know by now, the correct answer is a. It might seem odd to step up your enforcement by backing off, but that's exactly what you should do around food. Insist that your child sit at the table, and that he sit properly, but don't force him to eat. Like any other situation where expectations are established and communicated, mealtime should be about choices and consequences. Set the expectation that this is dinner, it's time to sit and eat, and if your child chooses not to, tell him there's nothing else until the next mealtime.

☑ Is your child a healthy weight?

If I see an overweight child, I see a problem in immediate need of a solution. We all know obesity in children has grown more common. In fact, 43 million children under the age of five are overweight or obese.* While we can point the finger everywhere, from commercials to less recess time to what the lunch counter is serving, parents must take a hard look at their family's habits and views around food, as they are primarily responsible. Obesity sets children up for pitfalls in every way, from self-esteem to sports and to the ability to make healthy choices the rest of their lives. I don't want children dieting, but I want them learning about healthy choices. Here are the excuses I hear most frequently from parents of overweight children, and my responses:

Excuse 1. My child won't eat anything other than junk food!

That's ridiculous! Offer them healthy food and if they don't eat it, they don't eat. Don't overcomplicate it.

Excuse 2. I'm so busy, I get home from work and don't have time to cook a healthy meal.

It's hard, I know. There is a lot of organization required so that you can both feed your child a healthy meal and be sane. I think I've made clear by now that I don't want parents to martyr themselves, and there are many (positive) shortcuts on the road to healthy eat-

* www.hsph.harvard.edu/obesity-prevention-source/obesity-trends/global-obesity-trends-in-children.

ing. I've sprinkled some tips throughout this chapter, but some of my favorites are to make food in bulk so that you can freeze some of it and have it on hand later. Spaghetti Bolognese is a great example of such a meal. Or you can pick up a rotisserie chicken from the market and toss some broccoli into the microwave.

3. My grocery budget is stretched as it is—I can't afford the healthier options.

You do not have to feed your children organic sirloin steak in order to feed them more healthfully. Inexpensive and healthy options include minced turkey, potatoes, frozen peas, and whole-grain pasta. Shepherd's pie is one of my personal inexpensive favorites. Or start with the cereals in your pantry: sugar cereals cost the same as low- or no-sugar cereals. Read the label and make the better choice. Plus, if you don't spend your money on healthful food, you will be paying for insurance premiums or medical bills when your child is overweight.

4. I see my child so rarely, I want to make it special and involve treats.

Ah yes, parent guilt. There are appropriate times to show your children how much you love them, but you are doing them more harm than good by giving them bad food to eat.

☑ Does your child eat at regular intervals? Do you also avoid constant snacking?

I constantly see mums going out with their kids for a quick errand, and they run around beforehand packing a sippy cup and snack because heaven forbid their child go an hour without eating! "But he gets so fussy if he goes too long without a snack," they tell me. Or imagine this familiar scenario: You are out somewhere, say, the zoo, and your little one says she's thirsty and needs water. What do you do? Do you

a. pull the filtered water packs you've prepacked for just such an occasion out of the stroller;

b. leave the exhibit and make haste to the nearest fountain;

c. tell her that the next time you pass a fountain, she should let you know so she can stop and have a sip?

The answer is c. It acknowledges the child's feeling without catering to every whim. I am not suggesting that you shouldn't be prepared and organized—good for you if you are. But let's introduce some balance into our parenting. You are not facing the apocalypse—you don't have to have bottled water with you wherever you go!

The bottom line is that you don't want your children to be too hungry, but it's also okay to expect them to wait for food and not get a snack each time they have a hankering for one. **Parenting by being at your child's beck and call is exhausting, and does *not* make you a better parent. Quite the contrary!**

Reasonable increments for a child's meals vary depending on the child, his age, and your daily schedule. Often kids will have one or two meals in the day where they eat quite a lot (normally breakfast and lunch) and another meal at which they don't eat as much. You will know this about your child, and you'll know if he's being picky or if he's really not hungry. But as an example, the family I nannied for the most recently had an eighteen-month-old and a three-year-old. The boys ate breakfast at seven and lunch at noon. I would give them a snack at ten, but then found that if we skipped the snack, they ate more lunch and did just fine. I always gave them an afternoon snack after naptime—usually some apple and a piece of cheese. And then they ate dinner at around five or five thirty. This will vary for your family. Just make sure of two things:

1. that there's not too much snacking, and that snacks aren't so large that they substitute for dinner,

2. that your children are eating at regular intervals, so as to avoid blood-sugar meltdowns. Think of it this way: If you usually eat at noon, it's not a big deal for *you* to wait until one on a day when you have a lot of errands to do. Not so for kids. If you're not going to be home by their regular lunchtime, bring a snack or plan to stop. Note that this is very different from being a human vending machine, however!

BABIES AND FEEDING SCHEDULES

As you saw in the last chapter, there's a strong link between a baby's feeding schedule and sleeping schedule. A healthy infant should eat only every 2.5 or 3 hours. Here's why:

1. If you feed him on demand, he may begin snacking, and that's problematic. When babies nurse, the first thing they encounter is the foremilk. That's all well and good, but you also want them to be getting the hind milk. Whereas the foremilk has mostly lactose, the hind milk has lactose *and* fat. He will be less hungry if he gets the hind milk, and he'll be getting more of what is essentially the perfect food. It's a similar theory with older kids: If they snack all day, it's harder to get them to eat supper, which is where you're serving the best options.
2. If you do a good feeding every 2.5 to 3 hours, you are more in control of the schedule. You can feel confident they've had a full feed. You must start with a baseline, after all, to know when something is amiss. In this way, a routinized feeding schedule can help you learn your child's cry. When you then wean him off of nighttime feedings, it's much easier to do because the question of whether he's hungry or not is determined.

Which all begs the question of how, exactly, you *resist* feeding on demand. There are some excellent tricks. If your baby eats a little bit but then loses interest or, more commonly, falls asleep, then you can undress her. The cold air will make her a little chilly, which will perk her right up and likely make her want to have a go for some more milk. You can also tickle her face. Another favorite trick of mine is to put a damp, cool washcloth on her face and body.

Now, if the problem is not that the baby loses interest but that she seems to want the breast or bottle again soon after she's had a good feeding, then what? Three words: *Resist the shortcut.* Don't assume that just because she's fussy or rooting that she is hungry. She may just want to be comforted, and while the breast or bottle is surely the easiest way to comfort her, resist. Rock her, pat her, give her a bath, and give her a pacifier if she's less than three months. If it's daytime, take her for a walk in the fresh air.

Remember, mums, your boobs are not pacifiers! So often parents just put babies on the breast when they cry, and really most of the time they're crying because they have gas. When gas is the problem, give her a tummy massage, move her little arms and legs about, and try pushing her knees into her chest. If you're breastfeeding, keep a food diary to see what baby might be reacting to. Broccoli, strawberries, and chocolate are particular culprits, but don't cut them out (especially the chocolate, for heaven's sake!) until you've drawn a connection between the food and your baby's gas. Take out one food at a time and see if that helps your baby. Remember, *more* milk just exacerbates the problem of an upset tummy, so the cycle goes on and on.

I do not think anyone need be completely rigid about a feeding schedule. If it's fifteen minutes before the usual feeding time but your child is hungry, by all means, feed him! Or if you are going to be out and about and can't feed him until a bit later than usual, of course, do what you must. Think of schedules as helpful tools, not as handcuffs.

☑ Does your child sit down to eat?

Where a child eats says quite a lot about her relationship with food, and your expectations around meals. Does she routinely eat in the car? I will be the first to admit that I have fed children in the car. Sometimes your schedule means that you have to, especially if you have older kids. I don't think it's a good practice, plus it's a choking hazard, but if you need to make exceptions sometimes, so be it. However, make it an exception rather than the rule, and teach children that food is about much more than just fuel.

I can't stand seeing kids running around eating food. It's bad manners, for one, which I will go into much more in the next chapter. Second, you don't want food all over the carpet and furniture. Third, it's a choking hazard. Other parenting guides would disagree with me. "You just want your kids to eat, it doesn't matter how or where!" One expert explained how toddlers like to move around and graze. Well, they're not cows! They're little people and they need to learn to appreciate food properly. To be fair, your child *will* probably eat more if you let her eat on the go. But she's also not learning to listen to her body. I know that I can eat an entire bag of kettle corn by myself while I'm watching the TV, but that doesn't mean I should. Setting such an expectation is not that difficult.

And under no circumstances should you allow your child to eat on your lap! The next thing you know, she will only eat on your lap. There are plenty of times to hold and cuddle your little one, but mealtimes are not one of them. Teach her good habits by teaching her to eat in her own chair.

☑ Does your child have good table manners?

My nana was a stickler for manners at the table. "Sit up straight, Emma," she'd say. "Watch your posture—shoulders back." Elbows were always expected to be off the table, and it was absolutely unacceptable to eat with your mouth open.

Nana's lessons stuck with me. I can't bear to eat across from a friend who doesn't close her mouth when she eats, and I even broke up with a boyfriend because I couldn't get over his eating style. It just put me off my food—and killed my attraction to him in the process. It astounds me how frequently people eat with their mouths open. We have lips—close them! No one wants to see a bunch of chewed up food rolling around. It appalls me that people haven't learned this basic manner.

Mealtimes are an excellent place to begin teaching manners. For instance, a child as young as eighteen months old can learn to clear his plate after a meal. And older children should learn there is to be no technology at the table. Bringing your cell phone along shows disrespect for your eating companions, your food, and whoever has prepared that food. Though I will get into manners much more in the next chapter, here are my top eight mealtime musts:

1. Sit up straight—no slouching!
2. Keep your legs under the table.
3. Use utensils (children as young as eighteen months can do this).
4. Cut up food (you can do this for them if they're small, of course).
5. Eat with your mouth closed.
6. Don't talk with your mouth full.
7. Ask to please be excused.
8. Say "thank you" for the meal.

I will be the first to admit I might be a little strict in this arena, but is being civilized really so bad? I was taught to respect my food, my eating companions, and the ritual of mealtime, and I'm constantly grateful for it. I would much rather be teased for my impeccable manners than for eating with my mouth open. Which would you rather have your child be teased for?

Note I do not think we need go back to the days of *Downton Abbey*, where we would eat with ten different utensils each night just to be proper. Mealtimes need not be that ritualized. I don't even think there's anything wrong with putting the butter container directly on the table, provided you're not having guests over. But we also don't need to be slouching in front of the TV with melted cheese hanging off our chins. Let's find the balance.

☑ Do you limit the amount of sugar in your child's diet?

It will also come as no surprise that there is too much sugar in our children's diets, but sometimes it's hard for parents to see the connection between diet and behavior. A family I know of from the former Soviet Union struggled with overwired children who went to bed much too late at night and struggled to get up—and behave—throughout the day. When it was pointed out that the children drank black tea after 8:00 p.m., the mother laughed. "We're Russians," she said. "We can handle tea." While most Americans would clearly see the connection between black tea and insomnia, Americans have their own cultural assumptions, and seem blind to the connection between sugar and poor behavior. I once worked with a mum who struggled to get her hyperactive young boys under control, and though she tried everything, she didn't think twice about offering them Popsicles for breakfast. Sugar cereals remain a huge and all-too-common vice, and even savvy parents can have difficulty making sense of labels and determining what's really nutritious.

On this point, be very cautious about juices and flavored milks. Jamie Oliver states that kids in the United States can consume eight pounds a year of added sugar just from flavored milk! Both juices and flavored milks are marketed as healthful, but are often packed full of sugar. Is sugar or high-fructose corn syrup the first ingredient? If it is, don't purchase it, or at the very least consider it a special treat and not just part of a regular meal. I find peanut butter to be a great and healthy snack but also encourage parents to use caution about how much jelly they add to their child's PB and J. The more natural, low-sugar jelly you can buy, the better, or better yet, mash up strawberries or bananas to add to the peanut butter sandwich and do away with the jelly altogether.

I've consulted with parents of many, many hyperactive kids. The children have difficulty controlling their behavior, difficulty settling down to do their homework or to rest at night. They are great kids and perhaps their parents are doing everything right, but they're also giving them a glass of juice with their after-school snack. No wonder the child can't settle down for homework! But again, sugar is such a ubiquitous part of the foods marketed and sold to us, we often miss the connection. I recently cut all sugar out of my own diet for a month. When the month was over, I binged and ate a bowl of jelly beans like it was my last meal on earth. My body felt awful afterward—not just that evening, but the whole next day. It was a worse feeling than the day after a pint too many (although as a side note, British ladies never drink out of pint glasses—only half pints, even if they have a dozen of them!). If that's the effect sugar has on me, imagine the effect on a little, growing body.

EMMA TIP

Be tough on sugar, but not so tough that you take away childhood rites of passage. It drives me nuts when, for example, on a child's birthday, the parent relents and lets him have half of a cupcake. It's his birthday! Let him have a whole cupcake!

☑ Are you offering a varied diet?

In one family I met, the parents explained that all the little boy would eat was bananas, string cheese, and chicken nuggets. "What do you mean?" I asked. I worried perhaps that was all Mum and Dad ate, too. I asked what they were eating. The parents said they ate a normal, varied diet. To which I couldn't help but wonder, *Who is the parent here? Who is in charge?*

If you provide your child watermelon, string cheese, and chicken nuggets for each meal, then of course he'll want it again. What does he know about a balanced diet? It's not good for him to eat in such a limited way, and it's up to you to provide healthy, balanced meals. It's fine to offer pasta with butter or chicken nuggets on occasion, even a couple of times a week. But when it becomes "all he'll eat," then the diet has ceased to be balanced. Offer your child protein, fruit, vegetables, and grains each day, and not the same ones. There will be a point when these parents cannot procure chicken nuggets, and then heaven help them!

☑ Do you prevent your child from filling up on beverages?

I've already said my piece about juice and flavored milk, but will say again that I firmly believe children should drink milk and water, and that's it. I will offer juice if a child is not feeling well, particularly if I'm concerned about him getting enough fluid. But juice should be reserved for illness and special occasions only.

Also be cautious not to give your child so much to drink that he fills up on it. I think it's fine to offer a glass of milk or water with a meal, but I do not permit a refill until all the food has been eaten. One family complained to me that their child wasn't eating, and I noticed he'd had four glasses of milk before his meal. Of course he wasn't eating! He was full!

EMMA TIP

I don't think *all* juice is bad—homemade juice can be wonderful! Relatively inexpensive juicers are available now, and I love them! You can open up the fridge and let your child select veggies and some fruit to toss in the juicer for a healthy drink. It gets kids excited about veggies, and is a great way to get rid of vegetables you don't have time to cook!

☑ Do you avoid removing "offensive" food from your child's plate?

Sometimes children will not like everything on their plate, and they must learn to deal with it. Parents frequently make this mistake because the requests start so small—Tommy doesn't want his hamburger bun or he detests carrots and doesn't want them near his macaroni and cheese. It's easy enough to remove the offensive food from the plate, and so we do. But it's a short road from removing Tommy's carrots to his having a meltdown in a restaurant because the server had the audacity to put carrots on his plate! The sooner you teach him to cope, the better.

Similarly, if your child doesn't want seeds in her melon, simply explain that that's how melon comes. If she wants to eat it, lovely. If she doesn't want to eat it, that's fine, too. Again, I know it sounds like a small request on her part. How difficult is it to scoop seeds off melon? But it becomes a big deal when kids see flecks of pepper in something and want it all picked off. Parents ought not be pepper pickers!

☑ Is your child aware of what he's eating?

There is a phenomenon lately wherein cookbooks suggest ways you can trick your children into eating healthy foods. We make cookies with spinach in them, or milkshakes with eggs, like Fudge's grandma did. I don't agree with hiding foods. Kids need to see what broccoli looks like, what peas look like, and learn to respect them, where they come from, and of their importance from an early age. Kids need to understand their food sources. Food can still be presented in a fun way, of course. I make green macaroni and cheese all the time, where I blend spinach into the mix. But the children know there's spinach in there— in fact, they help me get it from the fridge and blend it all together. Putting a happy face on a sandwich or waffle is silly and fun, and perfectly appropriate. Just make sure kids know what they're eating.

☑ Are you a good role model around food and nutrition?

You cannot expect your child to eat in a proper way if you do not do so yourself. If your children see you reading your mobile phone texts at the table, or filling up on potato chips right before a meal, they will want to do such things, too. If you make food for yourself separate from what you give your children, they will get the message that they have a choice about food and do not need to eat what's in front of them. And if you don't eat *with* your children, you are denying them the opportunity to learn by your example. Understandably, both parents may not be able to eat with the children each evening, but children should eat at least one meal a day with an adult, whether it be breakfast, lunch, or dinner, and whether it be with just one parent or even a nanny or babysitter.

EMMA'S GUIDE TO QUASHING MEALTIME THEATRICS

Throwing food. Around twelve months, if not earlier, children will do this. They think it's a game. Here's what you do:

1. Offer a warning. Say, "Tommy, if you throw your food again, I'm going to take it away."
2. Follow through when he does in fact throw it again. "I'm taking your food away because you threw it. But you need to sit there nicely while the rest of us eat."
3. If he calms down and begins behaving, offer him his food again.
4. If he throws it again, repeat steps 1 and 2.

Mealtime tantrums. A little boy, Daren, was eighteen months old when I nannied for him and his three-year-old brother, Jake. I served both boys plates with noodles, broccoli, carrots, and pork. Daren ate only the noodles (sound familiar?) and threw some food on the floor. I told him he was not to throw his food on the floor again, or else I would take it away. He threw it again, and I took his plate away. Then his brother and I proceeded to eat the rest of our meal while Daren screamed. We just ignored him and he calmed down. (Sometimes, if the crying is really disruptive, I recommend parents pop the child on the floor and see if that helps, but generally you want him to stay in his seat so he understands mealtime is a time to sit at the table.) When Jake and I finished eating, I cut up a pear and gave Jake some of it. Daren went bananas. He wanted pear, too. I told him he couldn't have it because he threw his food and was all done. I wasn't trying to rub in the fact that Jake got pear while Daren didn't, but I wasn't going to hide it, either. Daren was old enough to learn cause and effect: Both boys had a choice about what to do with their dinner. Jake ate his nicely, and so got some pear. Daren didn't, and so he went without.

EMMA TIP

Involve your child in the food-prep process as much as possible! Let her help you make a grocery list, and take her with you to the grocery store. If she's old enough, she can hold the list and help you find items on it. See if there's a new vegetable or other healthy food she wants to try, and allow her to put it in the cart. Then let her help you as you prepare the new food at home—even if you are just talking through what you're doing.

☑ **Do you monitor the quality and quantity of snack food available?**

Keep snacks out of young children's reach. At two, they should not be able to open the snack drawer and pull out crackers for themselves. When they're older, they may be able to access snacks more easily but they should ask before they take anything.

Snacks should be as healthy as possible, and I strongly encourage parents to limit the amount of sugar in the home. Cheese, apples, nuts, crackers, peanut butter, edamame, hummus, and carrots are all excellent snacks. Yogurt tubes can be popped into the freezer, and come out as Popsicles (though watch the sugar content—some yogurt is full of it!). Or try dipping strawberries in yogurt and then putting those in the freezer.

PARENT TIP

We buy plain yogurt and mix in fruit or a fruit puree pack. Our kids love it and it gets them used to what yogurt *should* taste like.

☑ Are your expectations reasonable?

Raise the bar for your children and expect them to behave appropriately, but don't expect them to sit nicely through four courses or more at a fancy restaurant. That's an unreasonable expectation (even for many adults!). At more casual restaurants, I encourage parents to bring crayons and paper for little ones. And don't expect your three-year-old to appreciate sushi straight off the bat or to eat spicy foods. It might be years before the taste for these foods is acquired, and it would be unreasonable to expect otherwise.

☑ Do you offer incentives such as dessert, but not too often?

Some think it's an unhealthy bribe for parents to say, "If you eat your dinner, then you can have dessert." I would argue that that isn't a bribe, but rather teaches healthy eating habits. You are teaching your child that once she gets all of her nutrients, then she can have dessert, but that it's not healthful to fill up on sugar alone. Isn't that the way most grown-ups handle it? If I fill up on chocolate, I don't want dinner, and usually I feel terrible later; that's why I'm (usually) pretty good at having my chocolate *after* dinner. Incidentally, dessert doesn't have to be chocolate or cookies—fruit is a perfectly acceptable after-dinner treat.

Also, it's important to let kids be kids. You want them to have a normal upbringing, which involves birthday parties with cupcakes and other treats. Kids should know what cotton candy tastes like—as well as hot chocolate on a cold day. They should know the satisfaction that is a hard-earned bucket full of Halloween candy. If desserts are treated as treats, and not part of an everyday diet, then they are fine!

☑ Do you give your child a choice?

Offering a choice does not mean asking "Would you like broccoli or pizza tonight?" But it is important to remember that children like to feel in control of decisions in their lives. When it comes to eating, let's face it, unless you are willing to force-feed them—which I would not recommend—they *do* have control. My favorite techniques for offering choice include the following:

- If your child isn't eating, divide the food on a plate into two portions—a larger one and smaller one. Ask your child to choose which side he's going to eat. Chances are, he'll pick the smaller side. He'll feel like he's in control and will be happy to eat, and you'll be happy he's eating at all.

- Allow your child to choose which vegetable to have with dinner (again, limit the options to two or three).

- Get your child involved in preparing the meal. He can measure, stir, or control the timer. There's plenty to do that doesn't involve knives or fire, and it will help him feel in control.

PARENT TIP

One of my kids' favorite meals is "make-your-own soft tacos." Everyone gets a soft tortilla and picks his own toppings (black beans, Cheddar cheese, tomatoes, grilled onions). It also works well for "burrito bowl" night, with rice as a base and lots of toppings to choose from.

☑ Do you routinely introduce new foods?

The more you feed your child the same flavors, the more he will have a taste for them, and in this way I believe Americans' love of sugar starts very young. American parents introduce their babies to blended fruits like applesauce and pear sauce, and then keep them on the fruit sauces for ages. In England there is much more emphasis on giving babies blended vegetables, and a wide variety of them at that. Regularly introduce new tastes, and they will develop new tastes. Also, don't make a big deal of giving children something new for dinner. Going on about how much children will love beets or some such is apt to make them suspicious. However, you can let them choose a new vegetable at the grocery store to try. You can also get them excited about trying foods from different cultures, like pad Thai or dim sum. You can make it fun by combining the new food with information about the culture it came from. There's a difference between genuine excitement and empty enticement, and they will be able to sense it.

☑ Do you persist if your child doesn't like something the first time he tries it?

Experts say that a child needs to taste something as many as twelve times before he can determine whether he likes it or not.* Some tastes are absolutely acquired, so don't give up. And if there is something that your child will not eat, such as mashed potatoes, don't give up on serving them to the rest of the family just because he won't eat them. That sends the message that he determines the menu, and that is not a good message to send. He may not ever eat them, but as long as you enjoy them, keep preparing them and presenting them!

---

*Dawn Drzal, "You're Invited to Dinner with Dr. Oz," Oprah.com, August 10, 2011. Retrieved August 26, 2013, www.oprah.com/food/Dinner-with-Dr-Oz-and-Family-Vegetarian-Cooking/2.

☑ Do you avoid food games?

Playing games to encourage children to eat is a nice idea, and I've certainly engaged in my fair share of "Here comes the plane—whoosh—open wide!" But who has the energy to do that every day? Before you know it, you'll be performing cartwheels for your child to eat carrots or doing push-ups for peas! You may laugh, but people go to extremes to get their children to eat. Cut the drama and make the food the main event.

☑ Are you trusting your instincts about your child's weight?

Parents sometimes see it as a personal failure if their child is too slender. They are prepared to move heaven and earth in order to get their child stuffed with calories, and they look at their child's placement on a growth chart as a challenge. There are some children who are unhealthy and underweight, and doctors and parents have good cause to be concerned. But trust your instincts on the matter, not just a weight chart. There's nothing wrong with being in the tenth percentile, or even the zero percentile—someone must be; otherwise how would there be a chart? If you or the child's other parent was small as a child, that may be why your son is slight. If your child's weight drops suddenly, that's a cause for concern. But if not, as long as he's active and sleeping well, gaining weight, even if slowly, and healthy in all other respects, don't use just a growth chart to determine if he's eating enough. Let it go. Understand that we live in a culture of "more is better!" and fight that urge to feed your son ten ounces of milk even if he seems satisfied with six. And do not put formula or protein powder in baby's breast milk, as some pediatricians suggest! I hear of pediatricians doing this all the time and I think it's simply crazy. Unless your child is malnourished, trust your instincts.

Bon Appétit

I'm so delighted to have shared my findings about food because it's an area where parents can make their lives easier and their children's habits healthier by doing *less*. And it's never too late to start new habits. Remember that the most important thing you do when it comes to your child's nutrition is to back off. Unless there's a medical problem, children are excellent at eating exactly as much as they need. As long as you're providing varied and healthy options, they'll get the nutrition they need. If you can let go of trying to control how much they eat, mealtimes will be more pleasant for everyone.

Nutrition and mealtimes have such potential for improving other areas of a child's life and behavior. Proper nutrition improves sleep, for one. Mealtimes are great opportunities for sharing quality time, which I'll discuss in Chapter Nine. And dinner can also provide a wonderful chance to teach your children manners, which is the subject of our next checklist. So elbows off the table, please, and let's begin.

CHAPTER FIVE

Little Lords and Ladies

Manners and Respect

"Respect for ourselves guides our morals; respect for others guides our manners."

—Laurence Sterne

CHECKLIST

☑ Does your child refrain from interrupting?

☑ Are you developing patience in your child?

☑ Are you developing generosity in your child?

☑ Does your child ask for things properly?

☑ Does your child treat his things well?

☑ Does your child behave well around his peers?

☑ Does your child treat her siblings well?

☑ Does your child respect her elders?

- ☑ Does your child respect **you**?
- ☑ Are you clear about who's the parent?
- ☑ Does your child behave well in public settings?
- ☑ Does your child appear presentable?
- ☑ Does your child have proper mealtime manners?
- ☑ Are you teaching your child empathy?
- ☑ Does your child understand and say he's sorry?
- ☑ Do you enforce manners?
- ☑ Does your child express gratitude?
- ☑ Does your child greet people properly and say good-bye properly (or at all)?
- ☑ Are you a good role model?
- ☑ Are you polite with your children? Do you speak to them with respect?
- ☑ Do you respect your child's body?
- ☑ Are you respectful of your own things?
- ☑ Is your language appropriate?
- ☑ Do you have realistic expectations about what your child is capable of?

RECENTLY I WAS driving north on Interstate 5 from Los Angeles to San Francisco. It's a road I travel often, and, as usual, it drove me bonkers that people drove in the far-left lane instead of just using it for passing. Fortunately, I ended up getting behind a guy in an Audi who shared my habits. He kept shifting to the left lane to pass a slower car, then back to the middle lane, then back to the left to pass a slower car, and then back to the middle. I followed him practically the entire way. *He must be British*, I thought, and when he finally exited, I gave him a little salute.

In Britain, you take care not to slow down other drivers. Hence, the passing lane is actually used as a passing lane. A driver in Britain would never dream of staying in that lane. In America, the etiquette is different, and while it may seem like an innocent enough difference—a habit and nothing more—it's very revealing. Why aren't American drivers concerned about others on the road? It's like they're all so anxious to hold on to their piece of pavement, there's no room for courtesy. It's the same way on escalators. In airports across the country, travelers stand in the middle of the escalator and no one can get by. If you ride the Tube in London, on the other hand, all of the pedestrians stand on the right side of the escalator on their way down to the platform. They wouldn't dream of standing to the left as they might block someone trying to get past. And don't even get me started on the difference between American and British queuing habits! If I sound harsh, it's because when it comes to manners, the British solidly take the day. I'm sorry, but that's the truth.

It's been that way as long as I can remember.

My stepfather is a member of the Royal Air Force Police, so I grew up on British military bases where American families worked alongside the RAF. Every time we relocated to a new town, my brother and I would seek out the American kids on base. We loved hanging out with them because Americans were the most fantastic playmates. They were fearless, defiant, disorderly, and confident. They had all the cool toys and gadgets. They would blurt out answers in class while the British students had to follow the unwritten rules of raising their hands to get permission to speak. They embodied all the characteristics that kids admire among peers, but not surprisingly, things that vex parents the most. I remember as a kid hearing the refrain, "Oh well, they're American," by the British parents when explaining the ill-mannered behavior of kids on the playground.

To be fair, I don't think the British are necessarily the most polite people around. That distinction would likely go to the Japanese. On some Japanese trains, the porters bow each time they enter a compartment, and bow when they leave it. Each compartment, each time! And when a client of mine and her husband were looking for a specific restaurant in Kyoto, the maître d' of a competing locale left his post so that he could personally walk them to their desired restaurant. Toilets in Japan are famously outfitted with noise machines, so that you needn't bother other bathroom users with the sounds of your personal business. Stories like this about Japan abound. Indeed, *domo arigato* ("thank you very much") is the most important Japanese phrase you will ever learn.

Unapologetic cultural stereotyping aside, there is nothing inherently wrong with American children that makes them ill mannered. **It's a phenomenon that has as much—actually, *more*—to do with the parents than the kids. Parents have gradually lowered the bar. They don't *expect* or teach their children to be well mannered anymore.**

When I was growing up, my nana and my mum were always correcting my speech and manners. They weren't just reminding me to say "please" and "thank you" but also to close my mouth while eating, to say "excuse me," to get up to give an elderly person a seat, or to stand up straight. My mum taught me how to carry myself in various situations, the importance of loyalty, of values and traditions, of responsibility and accountability. She set me up for success, not in monetary terms, but in life terms. I developed the necessary skills to make good choices, to push through when things got tough, to talk to people, to have and keep good friendships. **You**

aren't born with these abilities; you have to learn them, and it's a parent's job to teach them.

Lorraine is an Irish nanny, a friend I've known for years. I recently traveled to Boston to visit her and her charges who I first met when they were tiny. One of the children, Lola, who is thirteen, came in the house and saw me and Lorraine sitting in the kitchen. "Hi, Lorraine; hi, Emma!" Lola cried, and dashed upstairs. Lorraine was having none of it. "Lola, please come down here." Lola dutifully came down the stairs. "Lola, please come back here and say hello to Emma properly. You have known Emma for a long time and you haven't seen her in quite a while." Lola sat down across from me and proceeded to ask me questions about how I'd been. After we'd spoken for a few minutes, Lola excused herself and went upstairs to her bedroom.

Most parents and nannies I know wouldn't think twice about a thirteen-year-old hollering a greeting on her way to her private space. "She's thirteen, you know how it is," they'd say, or they'd even be delighted that she'd called out a cheery greeting instead of sulking upstairs without saying anything. That's a terribly low bar, and I believe it's time to raise it once more when it comes to manners. And the reason I feel so strongly about this is that manners are not an old-fashioned concept or habit best left behind with the times. Manners are fundamental. **Manners, in fact, have everything to do with respect.**

An ill-mannered child doesn't respect his toys, his friends, his siblings, or, worst of all, his parents. When I consult with a family having difficulties, I look carefully to see how their children treat the world around them. Do they think it all revolves around them? For instance, I once consulted with a mother of a three-year-old boy. This mother was a preschool teacher, and well versed in discipline techniques and common problem areas for children. But she could not take her son to playdates because he would act out. He was physically aggressive with other children and he threw toys. Running through my checklist, it was easy to determine that this boy's problems had everything to do with respect: respect for his mum, respect for his friends, respect for his toys, and respect for his own body. It was a problem this mum needed to resolve right away, before she became deaf to it. **While some parents become inured to their children treating them badly, I would argue that it is a very severe problem with repercussions in every area of the child's life. If kids don't respect their parents, then who and what will they respect?**

Parents today focus on their kids going to the best schools and doing the right extracurricular activities, but the most important thing on their list should be raising a respectful child, one with good morals and values—and that's the check mark we've lost. Children today learn to play soccer or the piano, but they don't learn to say "please" and "thank you," they don't look people in the eye when they talk to them, they don't offer their chairs for an older person, they don't chew with their mouths closed or wait until everyone's seated to eat. In this area, parents are failing their kids. They are not teaching them to respect those who inhabit the world around them, and this trait is at the center of so much else. Manners and respect will affect everything in a child's future, from whether he gets a job he interviewed for to whether he treats his spouse well. In other words, it's imperative to get this checklist right.

☑ Does your child refrain from interrupting?

All kids are going to interrupt, but I watch parents closely to see how *they* handle it. Teach your child to say "Excuse me" before they break into a conversation. Respond right away with, "Thank you for saying 'excuse me,' but I'm still talking. Please wait and I'll get back to you as soon as I'm finished." This simple response sends the message to your child that the world is not all about him. Do be sure to then always acknowledge when it's his turn. "Thank you for waiting so patiently. What was your question?"

☑ Are you developing patience in your child?

As you can see from the previous question, manners and patience are inextricably linked. Here are a few questions to help you gauge whether you're helping your child learn patience:

- When your child asks for a glass of milk, do you drop what you're doing and get it immediately?
- If you're talking on the phone and your child needs something, do you stop your conversation to get it?
- In the car, if your child is screaming for the radio as you're trying to negotiate a tricky bit of the road, do you fuss with the dials?
- If your child wants to play with a specific toy car that someone else is using, do you teach him he has to wait his turn, or do you find another car for him?
- If your child wants to leave the dinner table even though others are still eating, do you allow it?

If you answered an honest "yes" to any of these questions, then the next time you're in a similar situation, change your response. Show your children that they do not get whatever they want whenever they want it. It's never too late to teach them. There's only one exception: if you're potty training your child and she says she has to go, then drop everything and run as fast as you can to the loo. Barring this, make them wait to get what they want, and help them learn the invaluable trait of patience.

☑ Are you developing generosity in your child?

When it comes to generosity, it's the little things that count. If you are at the park with your child and a friend, and your child is eating a bag of chips, have him share them with his friend. If you have a friend come over to visit, or if your child does, get him in the habit of offering that visitor something to eat or drink. It's excellent practice, and breeds wonderful manners. Encourage your child to lend a hand to someone in need, but this comes along with teaching him good judgment about when it's safe to do so. An older child might help a mum move her stroller down steps. A younger child might pick up a pacifier or blankie that he sees another child has dropped. Though all very small things, they add up to a very large and important way of operating in the world.

☑ Does your child ask for things properly?

From the time a child can articulate "please," she should be saying it. In fact, the habit can start even earlier, with baby sign language. It's just a word, but it lays a foundation. Does your child often say, "I *want* . . ."? If so, respond with "I *want* doesn't get. Say, 'please may I' or 'can I please . . .' instead." The same is true for "I need . . ." Respond with "You don't *need*. You would *like* . . ." I can't stand a child demanding things—I find it terribly rude.

EMMA TIP

Role-playing is a great way to teach manners. One of my favorite activities is the old standby the tea party. Make it as elaborate as you like, with real food and tea or simply a toy tea set. Get dressed up (boys get into this, too, I promise!) and speak with over-the-top politeness. "Oh my darling, I'd love nothing more than a cup of tea! Thank you so much!" "Could I trouble you for a spot of butter for my roll? Oh, many thanks, this is delightful!"

☑ **Does your child treat his things well?**

Imagine this scenario: your child comes in from school, takes off his coat, and tosses it in the middle of the floor. Which of the following do you do?

a. Pick it up and put it on the peg. Normally you would ask him to do it, but he's just gotten home and is transitioning.

b. Tell him he needs to pick it up and put it in its proper place before doing anything else.

c. Leave it on the floor—he can get to it later.

The correct answer is b. It may be simpler to just pick up the jacket, or to wait for him to get to it, but you must look at the bigger picture. Think about the message that you'd be sending about respecting his things, respecting your house, and respecting you. **It's not just about a jacket; it's about respect.**

For younger children, the premise is the same. If I see a child throwing things about, like the three-year-old mentioned earlier, then he is behaving like a bull in a china shop and has not yet learned to respect anything other than his own desired movements. Teach him he must respect his things. A good teaching tool for some toddlers and preschoolers is jacketed books. In many households, if a children's book comes with a jacket, the parents discard it straightaway, knowing it will just become ripped. I disagree. If a child is old enough for a jacketed book, explain that the jacket is there to protect the book so that you can read it and enjoy it for years, and others can read and enjoy it once you're through. Explain that it's important to be careful with books and to take care not to rip the pages or the jacket. If the child rips the book jacket, he's not ready. Take it away, and try again another time.

Teaching children to respect their things teaches them awareness and responsibility. An eight-year-old boy I know went on a ski trip with his family and left his ski jacket in the rental car. It was an expensive jacket, and rather than replace it right away, the boy's parents told him he could not go on the next (daylong) ski outing because he didn't have his jacket. That jacket, they'd made clear, was *his* responsibility. Children will lose things occasionally, as we all do, but do you think that that eight-year-old boy took better care of his jacket when it was finally replaced? Absolutely. In contrast, a twelve-year-old I know lost his laptop. His parents replaced it before he even had much of a chance to miss it. When you replace lost objects as if it's nothing, you are teaching your child he can take things for granted. He will neither develop gratitude nor learn to take better care of his possessions.

☑ *Does your child behave well around his peers?*

At first glance, if a child isn't treating other children well—especially if he hits, kicks, or bites—it's easy to diagnose the problem as one of aggression. But I would argue it's more important to help the child recognize the following:

1. He is not the center of the world.
2. Other people have feelings, physical and otherwise, that can be affected.
3. And he must respect others.

If parents consider hitting and kicking acts of aggression, then they are missing the point. The child may learn to handle his physical impulses a bit more, but he's not learning the important values beneath *why* he must.

Children should also learn that sharing toys is a polite thing to do, and something they *must* do if they're having a friend over for a playdate. I always let children pick out one toy that they don't have to share, and they put it away in a cupboard before the playdate starts. But they need to share the rest of the toys. It's important for them to say "thank you for coming over" to their friends, or if they go to someone's home for a playdate, to say "thank you" to their friend for hosting and for sharing.

The park is another telling environment for whether manners and respect are a problem. Does your child pitch a fit if she has to wait for the swing? As with sharing, taking turns is a huge and very important lesson in manners, perhaps one of the first your child will—and must—learn. If the playground represents a battleground, do not ignore it and let your child get away with poor behavior. Take the time to teach your child the skills necessary to share the park with other children, or else she must leave the park.

☑ Does your child treat her siblings well?

Siblings will squabble, and for the most part I advocate leaving them be to work it out. They must learn to resolve conflict without you playing referee all the time. There are times when I will interfere, however: if one of them is still very little and needs protection; when there's name-calling; when one of them is speaking in a rude tone; or when there's any physical violence. Beyond that, you should talk about respecting everyone in the house at all times. Show them how to respect each other's space, and each other's bodies, then leave them be to sort out the rest on their own.

☑ *Does your child respect her elders?*

When I was growing up in England in the 1980s and '90s, the general rule was that any adult could reprimand any child. My behavior was fair game for criticism from everyone from my teacher to my friends' parents to the shopkeeper. As a result, I understood adults to be sources of power and deserving of respect. Whether my mum was present or not, I was accountable and I knew it. Today—both in the United States and the UK—we live our lives much more privately. What a child does in public is still a parent's private business. I'm not suggesting this is a bad trend, but I do believe it's had some negative consequences. Namely, our children don't show enough respect for adults.

In the past, sometimes the dividing line between adults and kids went too far in some British households, and I don't like that business about children being seen but not heard. Yet I think a middle ground is in order, as some children now speak to bus drivers, shopkeepers, and teachers in the most appalling way. I'm not so old-fashioned that I think kids must call adults "Mr." and "Ms." all the time, but if someone introduces himself as "Mr. Snow," the child should register that and call him as such. Doctors should be addressed as "Dr. So-and-so." Similarly, adults deserve to sit if there's only one seat available. In this day and age where children's needs so often seem to trump everyone else's, if you can teach your child to offer his seat to an adult, you're doing very well indeed.

> PARENT TIP
>
> I use children's books to help me teach my children manners—that way, it isn't all coming from me! *The Country Bunny and the Little Gold Shoes* is about a bunny who teaches her babies to take care of the home and pull their mom's chair out for her—the mom is considered "wise" for her teachings, and is chosen to be an Easter bunny.

☑ Does your child respect you?

A pediatrician I know is often galled when parents bring in their kids, and the kids will say something like "Shut up, Mom"—right in front of him! The mom will look at the doctor, embarrassed, and shrug. It's hard for this doctor not to intervene, and he often does, by asking the parents if they would like help regaining control over their children. (Which he does with finesse, somehow.) If the mum or dad says yes, they begin with respect. If a four-year-old is speaking to his mother that way, there is a problem that will only grow as the child does. It is never okay for a child to speak that way to anyone, let alone an older person or his parent. It should not be tolerated for a moment.

Tina Fey wrote in her humorous prayer for her daughter, "And when she one day turns on me and calls me a Bitch in front of Hollister, Give me the strength, Lord, to yank her directly into a cab in front of her friends, For I will not have that Shit. I will not have it."* Take inspiration from Tina and determine that you will not have that Shit (this is an important but necessary exception to the language rule—see page 132). Whether it's yanking her into a cab when she's a teen or taking him home from a playdate when he's a toddler, show your child that there are consequences for disrespectful behavior. **When we stop tolerating it, we raise the bar.**

☑ Are you clear about who's the parent?

This question ties in quite closely with the question above. If you are always trying to be cool and accessible to your child, he *will* say "shut up" to you. You haven't shown him that you are the parent, that you have the authority. This is not to say that you can't also be a

---

* Tina Fey, *Bossypants* (New York: Reagan Arthur Books, 2011).

kind confidante, a wise counselor, or a goofy playmate. **But you are always, always the parent. Your kids aren't always going to like you, and that's okay.** Indeed, if your kids always like you, you are doing something very wrong—trust me!

Two families were invited to my friend Holly's for dinner one evening. One of the visiting families included a nine-year-old boy who made wisecracks about the food when it was served. His father was sitting next to him and had a choice about what to do. Instead of sharply correcting his son's rude behavior, he laughed. This is a prime example of a dad who is more interested in being a chum than an authority figure. That son will not respect his father unless something changes. We mustn't allow this blurring of the lines. Our children need to impress us, not the other way around.

☑ *Does your child behave well in public settings?*

Kids who grew up with me in the UK were with their parents all the time, in restaurants, grocery stores, at friends' houses for dinner. We were treated like little people who could behave in an acceptable manner. We knew how to behave because it was expected that we *would* behave. Do you think twice about bringing your children along on errands or to dinner because you fear their behavior? If you resist bringing them, it's worth taking a hard look at why.

Most children have public meltdowns sometimes, so if your child does, that does not mean she is ill mannered. But on the whole, does she sit properly at a restaurant, understanding the code of conduct expected of her? Is she permitted to make music with her silverware and speak in a loud, inappropriate voice? Is she aware of the other diners around her, or does she think the world revolves around her and her alone?

A particular challenge with bad public behavior is that parents are so desperate to prevent a scene that they will do anything. Children know this. If your son wants a chocolate pudding, he'll wait until you're at a restaurant to ask, knowing you'll be more apt to give it to him in order to prevent a scene. Don't let your children's meltdowns handicap you. I will go into this more in Chapter Seven, but the key here is to put aside your fear of embarrassment and handle your child's behavior as you would if no one were watching. Other parents will respect you for drawing a hard line with your child, and if they don't, well, I would say they are part of the problem. We must support other parents, not judge them. It's far better for a parent to let a child tantrum in a grocery store than to give him the lolly he's been denied.

☑ Does your child appear presentable?

As anyone who has ever attended a job interview or nice party knows, appearances matter. I am all for letting children express themselves when it comes to their appearance, and care not a whit if they match when they go out, or if they combine polka dots, plaids, and stripes. But if they are going to a nice restaurant with

EMMA TIP

Some children are introverted, and it's difficult for them to look adults in the eye and say hello when greeted. Understand and cherish your child's inherent nature, but at the same time help her gain the confidence and skills she needs to interact properly with the world around her. She doesn't need to hug, kiss, or even give a high five to people if she doesn't want to, but once she's able to speak, she absolutely must say hello when spoken to. It may take many practice greetings and many reminders before she's able to do as you ask, but don't give up. Show her that she can continue being herself and keeping to herself, if that's what she wishes, while also greeting others politely.

you, they must brush their hair and dress appropriately. They don't have to match their socks with their skirts if they don't want to, but they should dress for the occasion; they must respect the rules and customs of the establishment they're visiting. **I believe in giving children plenty of room—if a behavior is not an issue of safety or respect, there's much I let go.** But there's also much that *is* about respect, and proper clothing for proper occasions is one of them.

☑ Does your child have proper mealtime manners?

I covered mealtime manners in Chapter Four, but I held back a couple of important, and I think revealing, stories. Once when my nana came to dinner, we had finished eating and were sitting at the table, the adults talking and the children not allowed to leave. (Another modern pet peeve of mine: American kids eating too quickly and then dashing away from the dinner table to play on their iPads or Wii's—or even worse, bringing their iPads to the table!) I was bored and decided to eat a few more buttered peas, so I stuck my fork into the serving dish. In an instant, my nana slapped my hand, accidentally hit the serving spoon, and catapulted peas everywhere. We all laughed uncontrollably, but I got the point. It's rude and unacceptable to reach out for food with your fork.

On another occasion, when my brother and I were acting up during a dinner, my mum forced us to eat outside at the garden table on the patio. "If you're going to behave like animals," she told us, "you can eat outside like animals." While I do not mean to suggest that you toss your kids outside if they misbehave, my mum raises a question worth asking: Are your children behaving like little lords and ladies, or like animals? Are they showing respect for you, the food, and the effort you took to prepare the meal? Mealtimes provide a wonderful opportunity to teach the importance of manners, so don't miss the chance.

☑ Are you teaching your child empathy?

Helping your child grasp that other people have feelings is a huge stepping-stone to teaching respect for others. The best way to teach empathy is to talk about feelings from an early age. Most experts say kids don't develop empathy until age four, but I've seen kids who are not even two go over to another kid who's crying and give a hug.

When reading a book to a toddler, you can say things like, "That monkey looks sad, doesn't he? Poor monkey! Do you think he's sad because he's missing his mum?" Or in real-life situations, say things like, "Tom is sad. Why do you think he's sad? How do you think we can help him feel better? Do you think we should ask him if he's okay, or if he needs a hug?" For older children, ask them to tell you stories about a gathering, reenacting the look on Granny's face when she opened a gift—the sillier and more exaggerated, the better! For two-, three-, and four-year olds, this is a great way to review feelings vocabulary and explore facial expressions associated with emotions. For slightly older children, this can lead to a simple conversation about being aware of others' feelings.

Ask your children questions: How did Granny look? How did the person who gave her the gift look? How did they, the children, feel seeing their loved ones so happy? And what will they do to help create that happiness the next time they participate in a gift exchange?

My friend Jessica and her husband recently watched a movie with their five-year-old daughter that contained a sad scene. The daughter said, "It makes me feel sad when I see a sad face. I don't know why." Jessica, who considered this one of her proudest parenting moments, teared up and said, "That's called empathy, honey."

☑ Does your child understand and say he's sorry?

I get into this more in later chapters, but "I'm sorry" is critical to at least touch on when we talk about manners and respect. If your child acts out and hits another child, he must apologize, but just as important, he must understand *why* he's sorry, *how* he has negatively affected someone else. You might say, "How do you think that made Eric feel when you hit him? . . . Right, not good, and I'm sure you hurt his body. How do you think it would make you feel?" This lays the basis for an apology that is more than just rote words.

☑ Do you enforce manners?

I have another pop quiz for you. Here's the scenario: You pick up your five-year-old from a birthday party at his best friend's house. He dashes out the door without saying good-bye to his hosts, or even "thank you." Which would you do?

a. Let him go, and thank the host and birthday boy on your child's behalf. After all, he's excited and wired on sugar—he couldn't possibly manage a thank-you.

b. Yell after your child and ask him to say good-bye, and deem it good enough when he throws up his arm, giving a half-arsed wave.

c. Ask your child to come back (even if you have to run after him and physically bring him back) and ask him to thank his hosts properly and say good-bye.

The correct answer, of course, is c. If you've answered a or b, don't despair—we've all let manners slip at one point or another, and it's never too late to begin enforcing them.

Enforcing manners is tedious, it's true. You may have to say hundreds of times, "Can you try that again?" or "Oops, did you forget to say something?" when your child doesn't ask for something properly. Remind children frequently to use the "magic word" and never give them what they want until they say "please" and ask nicely. Before a meal out or a dinner party at someone's home, remind them what the expected etiquette is. Let them know in advance that it's unacceptable for them to say anything bad about the food, even if they don't like it. If they are as old as four, I'd let them know that even if they don't care for the food being served, they need to take a few bites. And they absolutely must thank their hosts. Follow up afterward, if appropriate, letting them know they behaved perfectly with wonderful manners, and that you're proud of them.

A friend of mine had an embarrassing—if common—experience when her daughter was four. At Christmastime, an uncle gave the four-year-old a book as a gift, and when the little girl unwrapped it, she started to cry. It wasn't what she'd expected, she didn't want it, and she said so quite loudly. Mortified, my friend grabbed her daughter and took her out of the room. Quietly, alone, the mum explained to her daughter why her reaction was not okay, that she'd hurt the uncle's feelings and had not shown good manners. "Imagine how you would feel if you bought someone a gift, and spent time picking it out for them, and they reacted that way when you gave it to them?" The little girl was upset for a while, but eventually came back into the main room and thanked the uncle for the gift. The following day, out of the blue the girl said, "Mummy, I only said that I didn't want the book because I didn't know you're not supposed to say that." In other words, the experience was a formative one, an important one for the child's development. Ideally, the mum would have had this conversation before gift-giving time, but she rightly chalked it up to a learning Christmas for both of them.

☑ Does your child express gratitude?

> **EMMA TIP**
>
> Play a party game in which children pretend it's their birthday and open imaginary gifts. Help them to practice pausing after opening each gift, looking the gift-giver in the eye, and thanking him or her.

Saying "thank you" and sending thank-you notes are essential to good manners. Make it into a fun activity you can do together. If the child is very young, she can decorate a card that you write. If she is three or four, perhaps she can sign her name to it. If she's older, she can write it herself with some prompting. Even if the "thank-you" is just a phone call, enforcing it will show your children that it's important to feel, and to show, gratitude. Make sure to emphasize that gratitude is about more than enjoying the presents or party—it's also about being grateful for the people around us and the blessings in our lives. **Gratitude is what prevents the slippery slope to entitlement.** If you don't feel as though everything is due to you, you are grateful.

> **EMMA TIP**
>
> Thank-you notes needn't be an onerous chore. Perhaps create a box with construction paper, pens, glue sticks, and glitter, and label it "Gratitude box." When it's thank-you note time, your child will be excited to pull out the box. Or if you are writing your own thank-you notes, sit at the table with your child and write them out together, enjoying quality time in the process. Coach them to be as specific as possible—"I love my Lego and play with them every morning" is much better than "thank you for the gift"—but don't have them exaggerate their enjoyment of a gift, which sends them the wrong message about honesty. If the gift was a miss, they can write, "Thank you for the Lego. It was really nice of you to think of me and fun to see you."

☑ Does your child greet people properly and say good-bye properly (or at all)?

I once worked with a chef who used to always be so annoyed when the staff members would leave without saying "good-bye." "At the end of the night," she complained, "I don't know who's here and who's not, so I don't know who's expecting food or not." She was accustomed to working in Europe, where she said people were much more conscious about how their habits and movements affected everyone else, and it drove her crazy when her American colleagues popped in and out without a word.

> **PARENT TIP**
>
> Our son has his own stationery for thank-you notes, which he sends after every gift. He's only fifteen months old, so of course I write them, but he gets to add a slobbery kiss and we read them before sending.

Our children learn from us, and it's no surprise many are like Lola, my friend Lorraine's charge who I introduced at the beginning of the chapter. They'll pop through with a quick hello, if they say it at all. But I'd argue meaningful "hellos" and "good-byes" are small but powerful expressions, as are handshakes. When children are old enough (usually around four), they should learn the art of shaking hands with grown-ups, and should learn to do so confidently, making eye contact and adopting a firm grip. I have interviewed job candidates who did not look me in the eye or give me a firm handshake upon our greeting. Those subtle signs of a lack of confidence affected my view of them as much as their résumé and answers to my questions did. Perhaps confidence wasn't the issue at all; perhaps they'd just never been taught how to behave otherwise. But I perceived it as a confidence issue, and as in all job interviews, it's the interviewer's perception that matters. Granted, your six-year-old is likely not applying for a job anytime soon, but these habits start early.

☑ Are you a good role model?

I constantly see parents who yell or snipe at each other instead of speaking nicely, parents who order each other about instead of saying "please" and "thank you." Everyone has a rotten day from time to time, and there are times you will snap and not be at your best. But on the whole, if you are not polite to those around you, your child won't learn to be, either. If you are disrespectful to your barrista or the guy taking your order at the drive-thru, your child will not learn how to treat others and to acceptably behave and talk to people. Children mimic everything, and they will reflect the image you put out there, whether intentionally or not.

Before you wave off this check mark and pat yourself on the back for your always impeccable conduct, consider these instances of poor manners in adults that I witness all the time:

- If you're on the phone, and someone opens a door for you, do you stop your conversation in order to say "thank you"?

- Do you talk on the phone at the checkout counter? Some cafés and stores have signs admonishing patrons not to do this, and I think it's a wonderful reminder of basic manners.

- If your spouse or someone is telling you something, do you look her in the eye to show you're listening?

- Do you bring technology to the dinner table, or check your phone while you are at a lunch date?

- If someone lets you in in traffic, do you wave a "thank-you"? Do you let others in to traffic?

- Do you say "please" and "thank you" as a matter of habit?
- Do you chew with your mouth closed?
- Do you talk with your mouth full?
- Do you speak to others in a respectful tone?
- Do you hold the door open for others?
- Do you rsvp to invitations in a prompt manner?
- Do you interrupt others?
- Do you hold the elevator door open for others?
- Do you wait for everyone to have their food before you start eating?

If you are not perfectly mannered, don't worry, it's not that I'd think you were some sort of ogre! (Unless you always drive in the left lane on Interstate 5, which I've already said drives me completely bonkers!) Awareness is half the battle, really, so just take note and see where you go from there.

☑ Are you polite with your children? Do you speak to them with respect?

Think about it for a moment: The last time you asked your child to come to the table, what did you say? Did you say, "Come to the table, please," or "Come to the table!" If you needed something within your child's reach, did you say, "Can you pass me that bag, please?"

or "Pass me that bag," or "I need that bag"? The last time your child left food on her plate, did you reach over with your fork and take a bite, or did you ask first? The more you use your manners with them, the more they'll follow suit. It's that simple.

☑ *Do you respect your child's body?*

I touched on this in Chapter Two, but with younger children, respecting them means letting them know what you are doing when you pick them up. With older children, it means asking, "Can I have a hug?" "Can I pick you up?" If they say "no," you need to respect that "no." Kids need to feel like they have some control—and they should have control over whether they are cuddled or not. This is an important lesson for siblings to learn about one another as well.

Take this common scenario from a family I once worked with. The older sister, Kerry, was four, and loved to lie down on top of and hug her little sister. The little sister, Suzie, who was two, sometimes loved it, but sometimes she would cry. Had I told Kerry not to do it, she would have stopped, but she wouldn't understand the root of respect beneath the request. Instead I said, "It's nice to hug your sister, but you must listen to her, too. She's crying. She's not happy right now. You have to respect her body, and she doesn't want a hug right now."

The next day, the tables were turned and Suzie wanted to hug Kerry, who was not in the mood. "Emma, I don't want any hugs," she said.

I was trying to deflect the matter, so pushed Kerry just a little. "Just give her a hug and she'll leave you alone."

"No," she insisted, "I don't want one."

"Okay," I said. "Suzie, Kerry doesn't want a hug right now, but I'd love one. Can you come over here and hug me?" Suzie came over and hugged me, and the matter was resolved—if only for the day!

☑ Are you respectful of your own things?

Do you look after your belongings? Are your books thrown on the floor or neatly stacked in a pile? Do you look after your children's objects when they've entrusted them to your care? For instance, if they worked hard on an art project and you casually toss it into a drawer, that's disrespectful. I see so many kids crumble when something they made for their mum is shoved back in a drawer and not on display. Naturally, children create a lot of artwork, and you can't possibly preserve it all with care. But show them you respect their work by how you treat it in their presence. My mum still keeps a clay pig on her shelf, years after my brother made it for her. It's imperfect, and doesn't quite match the other objects, but she cherishes it and keeps it in a place of honor.

☑ Is your language appropriate?

Do you swear? If you do (which, let's face it, most of us do), be particularly mindful of not doing so in front of your children. Though my upbringing was very strict, when my mum and stepdad had a baby, they relaxed their vigilance a bit. When my baby sister was two, she was sitting at the table eating a digestive biscuit, and it fell off her plate and onto the floor. As the biscuit hit the floor, her tiny voice shouted, "Shit!" I'll never forget my mum looking at me with wide eyes. She wasn't accusing me of teaching my sister the word—my mum knew I never swore, because she'd never have tolerated it. No, my sister had learned the word from *her*. Mum was busted. Even in the most proper of British households, children will mimic their parents, and you must be as strict with yourself as you are with them.

☑ **Do you have realistic expectations about what your child is capable of?**

Children need a place where they can go out and be loud. Don't take them to a nice dinner if they haven't had the opportunity to blow off steam—kids can't use their indoor voices *all* the time. Don't expect a one-year-old to sit nicely and quietly at a restaurant, or even at the kitchen table for very long. And little kids—particularly boys—are going to find things like burping and tooting hilarious, and it wouldn't be fair to expect them not to. When your son burps and then laughs, don't make a big deal of it one way or the other. Do let him know that it's not acceptable at the table, but it is a natural function. Your role is to guide your children's behavior, but you must also let them guide you. Chances are good that you know when you'd be pushing too far, so honor that, and honor your child.

EMMA TIP

Ask your spouse, your friends, your colleagues, and your kids to call you out when you don't say "please" or "thank you." It might surprise you how frequently you forget!

A Proper Upbringing

Think for a moment about how critical manners are. We all know that bore at the party who must one-up every story anyone else has. Her sickness was worse, her trip was more exciting, her children are more accomplished. If she had any idea how she sounded to others, she'd stop talking at once. But she doesn't know, possibly because no one's ever taught her. Teach your children manners, and inoculate them from becoming the party bore.

We want our children to be confident, to feel like they can speak up and say if something isn't working for them. But we also

EMMA'S MANNERS MUSTS

I could write an entire book about manners! But there are a few essentials never, ever to forget yourself, and to encourage your children to adopt:

Basics

Mind your P's and Q's: say "please" and "thank you."
Get up to give your seat to an elder or a pregnant lady (basically anyone in more need than yourself).
Make eye contact.
Say "hello" and "good-bye."
Cover your mouth when you cough or yawn.

Dining

Sit nicely at the table.
Eat with your mouth closed.
Don't talk with your mouth full.
Wait until everyone has their food before eating.
Use utensils properly, *not* like a caveman!

Absolute No's

No interrupting
No talking over others
No climbing on furniture
No "pushing in" in a queue. Take turns!

don't want them to be entitled. I think Americans are wonderfully self-assured, and wish the British would learn to be more like them. And Brits do take manners too far sometimes, believe it or not. They are so vehement about the sanctity of the queue, for instance, that they are likely to view it rather rigidly and not allow someone to cut in if that person is genuinely in a hurry.

On the other hand, I think the British are more humble and appreciative of the gifts that come their way. So Brits, take some confidence from Americans, and Americans, please temper your confidence with better manners. As someone who has seen the best and worst of both of these cultures, I'd urge both to meet me in the middle, somewhere in the middle of the Atlantic.

CHAPTER SIX

A Time and Place for Everything

Scheduling and Routines

"Habit is the beneficent harness of routine which enables silly men to live respectfully and unhappy men to live calmly."

—George Eliot

CHECKLIST

☑ Does your child have a routine?

☑ Does your child know what that routine is?

☑ Does your child eat and sleep at regular intervals?

☑ Does your child spend enough time at home, but not too much time?

☑ Does your child have time to explore and use her imagination and creativity?

- ☑ Are you encouraging independent play, rather than being available at all times?
- ☑ Are focused activities part of the schedule?
- ☑ Is your child getting time outdoors?
- ☑ Is quiet time part of the schedule?
- ☑ Is active, physical time part of the schedule?
- ☑ Is your child able to focus well on activities like homework?
- ☑ Are you allowing enough transition time?
- ☑ Do playtimes and incentives follow task times?
- ☑ Are you limiting television?
- ☑ Are you limiting *all* screen time?
- ☑ Is whatever your child is watching or playing with appropriate?
- ☑ Are you flexible when you have to be?
- ☑ Are you okay with your child getting dirty, exploring, and running free (within reason)?

It hardly seems like the subject of schedules should be loaded or controversial—and certainly it's not when compared to sleep. Yet from what I've seen, parents tend to fall into two distinct camps on the subject. On one end of the spectrum, they resist "routine" as though it's a dirty word (and this happens particularly when their children are very small). They don't want to become rigid parents whose lives have been totally lost in deference to their baby's nap schedule.

They've always believed that if they kept a flexible schedule, their child would learn to do so, too, and would be more apt to go through life as a low-maintenance, go-with-the-flow sort, as apt to fall asleep in a crowded youth hostel as a fancy, quiet room. On the other end of the spectrum, you have the parents who embrace schedules to the point that they actually *are* pretty rigid about them. And then there are the parents who overschedule. "It's Tuesday, therefore it must be swim night." Their child is signed up for everything, and if there are too many free hours, parent and child alike feel disconcerted.

I don't think it's surprising that there's such a yin and yang on the subject. After all, parenting trends tend to be reactions to other parenting trends. The overscheduled parent is susceptible to pressures from schools and society that say "more is better!" And by the way, that message is absolutely everywhere. AT&T had a recent series of commercials wherein six-year-olds were interviewed on the subject of *more*. The children asserted that doing two things at once is better than one, that more is better than less, that faster is better than slower. The commercials are meant to be funny, but there's a pretty frightening undercurrent, and some parents are attuned to this dark side. These are the parents who take a step back from all the overscheduled children around them and decide they want to do it differently. They want entire days devoted to nothing but play, and see structure as the enemy.

To all this I say there's no need to be reactive; there's just a need to use good old common sense. As Oscar Wilde said, "Everything in moderation, including moderation." I am a big proponent of a well-thought-out schedule—children thrive with schedules and routines in their lives. At the same time, schedules also ought not be loaded to the brim. And I do not like schedules that don't allow for some deviation; chaos and changed plans are a normal part of life, and nothing teaches us this more than children.

Here are six reasons I love schedules, and think any parent who wants to make life easier should implement one:

1. Routine reduces chaos. Your children are less likely to challenge you, and more likely to cooperate, when they know what's coming and what to expect. It helps them feel secure, and eases the difficulties of transitions.

2. Routines help with setting boundaries. A good routine takes the enforcement of rules out of the parent's hands and into the clock's.

3. Routines simplify your day. A routine helps you plan, and also makes it easier to recognize a problem if there is one. In that way, it's like a scientific experiment. Keep factors like eating and sleeping the same, and you will be better able to isolate the reasons for behavior aberrations.

4. A good routine helps everyone meet his responsibilities. Children understand that they cannot have breakfast until they've fed the dog, and so a matter of routine becomes a habit. More work gets done around the house with less drama when those chores are part of everyone's routine.

5. A good routine improves family relationships, because time together is scheduled and therefore happens consistently, rather than fitting in around the edges.

6. Routines improve sleep, health, and literacy. In a study from Children's Hospital in Philadelphia, children who were put on a sleep schedule were much more apt to get more sleep than those who were not, and their mums were, too.* In a study from Ohio University, children

---

* Jodi A. Mindell, PhD, Lorena S. Telofski, Benjamin Wiegand, PhD, and Ellen S. Kurtz, PhD, "A Nightly Bedtime Routine: Impact on Sleep in Young Children and Maternal Mood," *National Center for Biotechnology Information*, May 1, 2009.

> who ate with their parents as a matter of routine were less likely to be obese.* And according to a study from the University of Nevada and the University of Missouri, the more regular the routines in the household, the more likely parents were to engage their children in literacy-enhancing activities.†

On every level—whether based in academic studies or practicalities—a good routine is a golden ticket. If you still have any doubt, consider that parents all over the country marvel at daycare's ability to get upwards of ten toddlers all quiet and resting at the same time. Part of their secret is expectation, as we've already covered, but with a heavy "assist" from schedule and routine. With the right tweaks, parents can create this at home.

☑ *Does your child have a routine?*

If I'm called in to advise a family about their child's behavioral difficulties, I study the child's schedule straightaway. I don't give parents a blank sheet of paper and say, "Okay, here you go, please sketch out his schedule." Rather, I ask them to keep a log each day of what exactly their child is doing at any given hour. It seems like a lot of work for Mum and Dad, but is well worth it. Often they think their child is eating, sleeping, and playing at regular intervals, but when they really look at the way it all pencils out, that's not so. A schedule's consistency is also key. Is the child's nap at noon one day, and

---

* Sarah E. Anderson, PhD, and Robert C. Whitaker, MD, MPH, "Household Routines and Obesity in US Preschool-Aged Children," *Pediatrics* 2010; 125:3 420–28; published ahead of print February 8, 2010, doi:10.1542/peds.2009-0417.

† Daniel J. Weigel, Sally S. Martin, and Kymberley K. Bennett, "Pathways to Literacy: Connections Between Family Assets and Children's Emergent Literacy Skills," *Journal of Early Childhood Research* 8 no. 1(February 2010): 5–22.

at three the next? Does bedtime vary as greatly? Do they have snack at nine on one day, then at one the next day? How much variance is there? Whether the children stay home most days or are in daycare, they need a schedule. Children with inconsistent schedules tend not to know whether they're coming or going. They feel ill at ease, and insecure. Step one is determining a schedule that works for your family, and keeping everyone true to it.

Routines are particularly important in times of change. The most common change I see is the arrival of a new baby brother or sister. Mum is home more, perhaps, as is Dad, and perhaps Grandma and Grandpa are around as well. Much about the older child's environment and world has changed all at once—he really has only an inkling of just how much!—and it's unsettling for him. Many parents, sensitive to their older child's needs and feelings, might keep him home from daycare or school during this time of transition. No, this is the worst thing to do. Send him to school like usual. What he really needs is the consistency of his routine to help him feel grounded and secure. Give him extra TLC, but don't add more change to his life by changing his routine.

I also see schedule inconsistencies when parents are particularly busy at work. One mum I worked for had a deadline and was away from home much more than usual. When she did get home, she lavished her son with affection, and because she felt so guilty about being away, she let him stay up later and wasn't as firm about setting limits. The little boy's behavior deteriorated—and in a major way. It was easy for me to see why. His mum was gone more, which set him on edge, but then she wasn't her usual self when she *was* home. His whole routine was out the window, which completely unhinged him. He needed extra attention from his mum when she got home, but he also needed her handling of him to be the same as always, just as he needed his routine to be the same as always. **In short, breaking routine will not ease your troubles or your child's—it will only add to the chaos!**

☑ Does your child know what that routine is?

I've said the drumbeat of communication can be heard beneath every single chapter, and we can hear it loudly when it comes to routines. The best routine is irrelevant if the child is unclear about what the routine is. For older children, write down the routine so that they can see it. Or better yet, involve them in planning the routine—kids like feeling in control. For younger children who cannot read, enforce the routine through consistency and verbal repetition.

☑ Does your child eat and sleep at regular intervals?

> EMMA TIP
>
> Allow older children to help set the schedule (within reason). That will help them buy into it and feel ownership.

While most children don't need naps by the time they've reached kindergarten, and can go longer periods of time without eating, for younger children these increments of rest and nourishment are key. If a child is always melting down at four and hasn't had anything to eat since two and won't eat again until five, it's likely he needs another snack. If a child sleeps thirteen hours each night but never takes naps, there needs to be an adjustment to your approach and the schedule so that he is able to take naps. See page 158–160 at the end of this chapter for age-appropriate sample schedules.

☑ Does your child spend enough time at home, but not too much time?

This chapter's checklist is all about balance and moderation. I don't like it when a child never has any time to spend at home. She's at school and then after-school activities and sports all week, and

PARENT TIP

Potty training was a nightmare with our three-year-old until we implemented a schedule. She would resist each and every time we took her to the bathroom, until we made bathroom times part of the routine. As soon as she woke up: potty. Before leaving the house: potty. As soon as returning home: potty. The more she got used to sitting on and using the toilet as part of her daily rhythms, the more she was willing to use it.

perhaps doesn't get home each night until shortly before bedtime. Then the weekends are similarly packed with trips and playdates and activities, so that she's lucky if she gets to spend a single waking hour a week in her room. Though there isn't a formula, you want to find a balance. If your child wants to join a soccer, swim, or hockey team, great—but not all three of them! Kids need a few nights a week where they can just be kids. They need time and space to do their homework, eat dinner with the family, and just chill.

On the other end of the extreme, I don't like to see children who are homeschooled and also home most of the weekend. They are not getting to experience and interact with the world enough, and they are not learning very valuable social skills. Most parents know the value of not spending too much time at home because, simply, their children tell them. They are climbing the walls, and so are Mum and Dad, until everyone piles into the car or around the stroller for an outing.

☑ *Does your child have time to explore and use her imagination and creativity?*

Self-directed play is so important to children, and there are few things more satisfying than listening to a little one lost in a world of his own making, filled with knights and princesses and talking dinosaurs. And it turns out that such activity plays a critical role in a child's development. According to the *New York Times*, "Studies suggest that free, self-directed play in safe environments enhances resilience, creativity, flexibility, social understanding, emotional and cognitive control, and resistance to stress, depression and anxiety."* The article explains that young children are particularly open to different ideas, probabilities, and philosophies when solving problems—an excellent trait! But it's also a trait that peaks when the child is about four or five. Then what happens? Well, think about it. When do extracurricular activities typically begin in earnest in a child's life? When do the hours of free-play time decrease? That's right—around the time they start school.

So again I'd ask you to look closely not only at how many structured activities the child has going on at once, but how much time is taken up by those activities. If a mum or dad tells me "Oh, my daughter only has school and piano, and that's it," that doesn't seem like a lot. But when I see the schedule written out, I see that their daughter gets home from school at three thirty, has a snack and then practices the piano until dinner, and then does her homework after dinner until bedtime. Where does she have time to use her imagination and creativity? She must follow instructions all day at school. Then she must follow the notes and structure of her piano lessons, then the structure of her homework assignments. When in her day does she get to sit at the kitchen table and color? Or dance around and be silly? When does she get to free her mind to come up with her own original thoughts, instead of following others'? The bottom line: kids need free time!

---

* David Dobbs, "Playing for All Kinds of Possibilities," *New York Times*, April 22, 2013.

☑ *Are you encouraging independent play, rather than being available at all times?*

If parents and other caregivers are constantly available to their child, he will not ever learn to play by himself. He will not feel comfortable exploring his own imagination without your help. He will not feel confident doing much at all without you. It's thus important to encourage independent play as a part of your child's schedule. Perhaps it's just for a short period of time at first, but then you can gradually increase it. Give your child your attention for a while, then get him involved in playing with something he's excited about. I'd suggest getting Lego or blocks and to start building something with him. Then say something like, "I'm going to go check the laundry and I'll be back in five minutes." Then make it longer and longer (assuming, of course, that your home is safe and baby-proofed). Sometimes he'll come see where you are before going back to his play, and that's fine. Build up the five minutes to ten. In time, you'll be able to have a cup of tea, put your feet up for a bit, and dream about the day you'll be able to ask your child to massage them. This independence is par-

EMMA TIP

Before encouraging independent time, fill your child with attention first. When they have a full tank, they will be more apt to play by themselves. Right when you get home from work, they will surely want your attention. This may be a tough time to give it to them, as you need to get dinner started, the dog fed, and the schoolbag unpacked, but it will help to either (1) take just ten minutes before you embark on dinner to really reconnect with them, perhaps by reading a book or playing a quick game, or (2) involve them with cooking dinner. Homemade pizza with premade dough is particularly easy to make with young kids' involvement, as is salad, considering they love to tear the lettuce.

ticularly important to establish when you are expecting a new baby. Your older child will want you when you're attending to the baby and physically not available to him; if he's never learned to play on his own, this transition will be all the harder.

☑ Are focused activities part of the schedule?

I worked with toddler triplets who absolutely ran wild all morning long. They had boundless energy and nowhere to channel it, so were constantly getting into mischief. Even a morning at home can be broken up into forty-five minutes of free-play time (ideally outdoors) followed by thirty minutes of a focused activity like working with toys and puzzles with Mum and Dad. Focused activities are fantastic because they facilitate one-on-one time with you. They teach self-control, and they help to grow a child's attention span. Further, focused activities encourage the development of gross and fine motor skills.

EMMA'S TOP FOCUSED ACTIVITIES

- Play-Doh
- Lego
- Building blocks
- Gardening
- Puzzles
- Baking
- Coloring or painting

☑ Is your child getting time outdoors?

Imagine this: It's raining. Again. You only have so many indoor rainy day activities up your sleeve, and your children are climbing the walls. For that matter, so are you! Do you

a. make hot cocoa and resign yourself to another day indoors—the weather will clear up tomorrow;

b. load everyone up in the car to go to the mall, where at least you can get an errand or two done and get out of the house;

c. pull out the raincoats and wellies, and do some serious puddle-stomping, followed by hot cocoa and a warm bath?

C is the best answer, hands down. The weather might *not* clear up tomorrow (remember, I'm from England, so I know these things), and going to the mall isn't going to drain anyone's energy except yours. Fresh air—even cold fresh air—is magic. Kids can get crazed if they're within four walls all day, and there's so much they can't do inside that they can do outside. They can kick a ball, they can be loud and boisterous, they can blow off steam and run around and be crazy. If your kids start to get fidgety or a bit crazed, open the door and kick them outside to play! (Not literally, of course.) Even if they're little, take them outside in the stroller for a bit of a reboot.

When I lived in Germany, I noticed parents would regularly bundle their children up and take them out for rigorous walks, even on freezing days. In parts of the United States, parents are much more resistant to being out in the elements. Interestingly, I've observed this more on the West Coast, where California families don't want to go out in the rain, but kids in Boston happily roll around in the snow. I know parents who take their kids on walks through their indoor mall on chilly days. It's good they're getting out of the house, I suppose, but getting outside would be even better. If it's snowing, put on their snow boots.

Fresh air can resolve a cranky mood, it helps release energy, and it eases sleep troubles. One family I know went on a beach vacation where they played outdoors all day, each and every day. Though in advance of the trip the parents were concerned about their young children sleeping well in an unfamiliar hotel room and all in the same room, sleep wasn't an issue at all. Naptimes were longer than at home, and at night the kids were asleep the moment their heads hit the pillow, with not a peep until eleven hours later. What's more, the parents were shocked at how much food their children consumed, and the pickiness of home was replaced by a ravenous hunger that had the kids eating everything in sight. Of course, we don't live our lives on vacation, but this can be seen as a test case of sorts. Add more outdoor time to your day, and see what happens.

☑ Is quiet time part of the schedule?

If your child is no longer napping, quiet time enables her to regroup her body, regroup her mind, and think about her day. Parents need it, too. Children aged three, four, or five should spend thirty to forty-five minutes a day in their rooms having quiet time. I don't care if they sleep, if they lie on their beds reading, or if they're in a corner rearranging their dolls. As long as they are quiet and getting some space for themselves, it's all that's needed.

☑ Is active, physical time part of the schedule?

Even if you think your child is getting enough exercise, it's worth a hard look. A recent study found that in just two generations, active play and physical activity have dropped by 20 percent in the UK, 32 percent in the United States, and 45 percent in China.* And yet

---

* "Childhood Inactivity Will Cost Your Kids 5 Years of Life," Designedtomove.org, report retrieved on August 26, 2013.

exercise helps kids cope with stress, focus, sleep better, and eat better. Why *wouldn't* we encourage it? The answer is simply that we're busy, and unless you have a large backyard and plenty of playmates for your child at the ready, ensuring your child gets time to exercise takes some effort. Though many elementary schools encourage recess and physical education, they are also pressured to meet high standards for testing, and gym and free play tend to be cut. And if parents don't see their kids until evening, when it's dark and there's much else to do, exercise drops off. So here's what I suggest:

1. Ensure the time your child spends away from you has physical activity worked in. If you have a choice between a school that protects recess time and one that doesn't, choose the former. If you have a choice between a daycare or after-school care that emphasizes fitness and one that does not, choose the former.

2. Make fitness time quality time. Once your child is old enough to move around, put a basketball hoop in the driveway or ride bikes in front of the apartment building. If it's too inhospitable outside, play a beanbag toss game, or Twister, or put on some music and have a dance party.

3. Make chores physical. Take a walk together to the store to get food for dinner (thus getting in your quality time as well). Have one of your child's after-school chores be running around with the dog in the backyard or raking leaves. Not all exercise has to be about fitness—it can also be simply about living and being active.

4. Model physical fitness. Let your children see you doing yoga stretches or sit-ups, or going for runs or walks. They'll understand exercise has an important value in your family.

☑ **Is your child able to focus well on activities like homework?**

The battle over homework is the one I hear about most often from parents of school-aged children. It's remarkable how a good schedule can make the battle virtually disappear. One six-year-old I worked with, Billy, had the most difficult time focusing on his homework. He would tackle it right after he got home from school, and his mum or dad would sit with him at the dining room table in an attempt to keep him focused—an attempt that rarely worked without an argument. Some simple schedule changes were all it took. Here's what we did:

1. Right when he got home from school was not the right time for homework. This was a little boy who had lots of energy! He needed time and space to blow off steam, and so we scheduled outside playtime right after school.

2. He also needed a healthy snack. Though it's easier for grown-ups to know that hunger distracts us, it's not always easy for kids to make that association.

3. Billy needed a consistent place to do his work, a space that was well lit and quiet, and that he would learn to associate with focused work. We got him a desk and a lamp and put them in a quiet corner.

4. Billy needed an incentive to focus and get his work done quickly, without Mum and Dad having to stand prison-guard style next to his desk. We decided that TV time would follow immediately after homework time. If he finished his homework, he would get the full allotment of TV time. If he missed it, that was his choice. (Note that Mum and Dad did check his work to make sure he actually

did it thoughtfully and did not just rush through it so he could watch TV.) The point is, it was on *Billy* to manage his time, and whether he got to watch TV or not was up to him.

Though the first day or two of such a schedule might incur a battle or two, by the end of the week, it will just happen. It's not magic, it's routine.

EMMA TIP

There are, obviously, differences in kids' temperaments as well as genders. If your daughter prefers to get her homework done right when she gets home from school, great! That obviously works for her, so there's no need to enforce a break when she'd prefer to get all her work done before play. I'll get into this much more when I cover trusting your instincts, but it's important to bear in mind that what works for one child won't work for another.

☑ **Are you allowing enough transition time?**

A mum reached out to me recently complaining about how her mornings were like a three-ring circus. Her four-year-old son was grumpy from the moment he woke up until he left the house for preschool. More than just wanting the mornings to run more smoothly, the mum also recognized that mornings and evenings were the prime times she got to spend with her son, and she wanted to enjoy them. Once I glimpsed the family's morning schedule, the problem was obvious. They were letting their little boy sleep until seven thirty, even though they needed to leave the house at eight. Though they put him to bed at eight at night, it was clear he needed more sleep than he was getting. Also, thirty minutes in the morning was not nearly long enough for him to transition from sleep time into school mode. There was also a lot that needed to be accomplished in that short period of time, so he was likely feeling his parents' pressure to hurry and their stress, which added to his grumpy mood. I suggested the following schedule instead:

THE NIGHT BEFORE

Before bedtime: Pick out clothes for the next day.

7:00 p.m.: Go to bed—early, I know, but listening to this child's signals, it was clear he needed more sleep.

THE MORNING OF

7:00–7:15 a.m.: Wake up and get dressed.

7:30 a.m.: Have breakfast.

7:45 a.m.: Brush teeth, put on shoes, and get schoolbag.

7:50 a.m.: Read a story with Mum.

8:00 a.m.: Leave for school.

I encouraged the mum to make sure her son knew the morning routine and expectations. She wrote out the routine and let her son decorate it, then put it up on the refrigerator. If, after a week of being consistent, mornings weren't moving any more smoothly, I told her she could try creating a sticker chart for her son. If each day he followed his morning routine without a fuss, he'd get a sticker for the chart.

☑ Do playtimes and incentives follow task times?

It's unbelievable how many families I visit where the kids are watching cartoons in their PJs while eating breakfast before school. Mum or Dad says, "Please get your school clothes on," and the child replies with, "I'm watching TV"—that is, if they respond at all! Why would you allow this as a parent? Giving the reward (TV time) before the child's jobs are done just makes your life all the more difficult! Perhaps this started as a habit that Mum and Dad are having a hard time breaking. Break it. If your child knows what his responsibilities are, and that he must get them done before he can watch cartoons or play, you will eliminate countless battles.

EMMA TIP

If a child is told to stay in bed until seven, set an alarm clock in his room. Teach him to tell time, or if he can recognize numbers, use a digital clock and teach him how to know when it's time to get up. For toddlers, use a clock that shows the moon and sunlight, and tell the child she must stay in bed until the sunlight shows up. These are great tools to empower your child to run his own schedule!

☑ Are you limiting television?

Let me say straightaway that I like television. I have fond memories of when I was a kid, and on Friday nights my family would get fish and chips from the local chippie and watch *The A Team* together. Television quality has improved since then, and on the whole tends to be more educational than *The A Team*. Further, when kids do watch some television, they are more apt to understand what their friends are talking about during recess. Before you scold me as a television proponent and peer pressure supporter, know that just because I'm not a television abstainer doesn't mean I'm not reasonable about it.

It all comes back to balance. First off, if your child is under two, she just doesn't need TV and may not be that interested. Leave it off. Second, if your child is out at preschool or school all day, then there's likely not much time in the evenings as it is. You have dinner, bathtime, and bedtime, and so if TV is part of the regular schedule, then quality time is left out, imagination time is left out. If your three-year-old is home with you all day, however, and you want to let her watch an educational show like *Sesame Street* for twenty-five minutes so you can get dinner on, I see no problem. As with so much else, as long as you don't overuse it, it can be a great and helpful tool. I also think it can be wonderful to make watching television special, such as having a family movie night with popcorn on the weekend, where the whole family watches a program together. (I personally love *Winnie-the-Pooh.* Being British, I believe it's in my DNA to adore it. I also love *Madagascar*, which is great for older kids and adults alike.)

☑ Are you limiting *all* screen time?

The lines between education and entertainment have grown blurry, and in some ways that's great. A little friend of mine informed me in precise detail what "vibrate" means, having learned it from *Sesame Street.* On the other hand, a mum worried to me about her mother-in-law's habit of putting the kids in front of math games on her iPad. "They're educational!" Grandma insisted. That may be so, but it's still screen time. It's still time the children are not interacting with you or using their own imaginations. Math games on the iPad are certainly better than music videos, but they still count as screen time. The reality is that the line gets blurry as technology becomes more and more accommodating of, well, everything. A good trick is to ask whether the function of the program is encouraging your child to think originally and freely. Some digital drawing programs can substitute handily when you don't have paper and crayons available. All that's different between drawing on the screen and drawing on the paper is the paper you've forgotten at home and that the restaurant isn't able to supply.

☑ Is whatever your child is watching or playing with appropriate?

Just as your kids will mimic your actions in the real world, they'll mimic what's on TV. And some kids are more sensitive to the sounds and images than others. Remain very involved with what your child is watching, and keep a close eye to possible links between a television program and a changed behavior, or a night of sleep that is less restful. Remember children are like little sponges, and are much more sensitive than you may realize to the stimulation around then. I have a friend whose father let her watch *Poltergeist* when she was five. He was so immune to such frightening concepts and images that he didn't fully absorb how much it was affecting his daughter. So strong was her fear then, that even though she's now a grown woman, she's never seen another horror film and refuses to. I had a similar experience with *Nightmare on Elm Street*, which I watched at a sleepover when I was thirteen. I was so frightened that I refused to sleep for days, and my mum was furious at my friend's parents for letting us watch it.

☑ Are you flexible when you have to be?

Be as consistent as possible with the schedule, but also give yourself the flexibility to change things up. Perhaps you always have dinner together, but what you eat isn't on any sort of rotation, and you are as apt to have picnics in the living room as take-out meals at the dining room table. Allow for some changes in timing, too. When you're establishing a new schedule is not the time to make an exception, but that doesn't mean exceptions shouldn't be made. Perhaps your toddler has her nap in the car when you're on a trip or picking up an older child from school. Sometimes you have to do what you have to do.

A family I know had a terrible time returning from vacation. The parents were busy catching up at work, the kids were off-schedule and discombobulated, and their behavior showed it, which only made the parents more stressed and exhausted, which only made the kids' behavior *worse*. It was a vicious circle, really. To this family, and the legions of families who have had just this experience, I say *relax*. Sometimes crap weeks like this will happen, but you mustn't be such a slave to schedule and routine that you don't go on vacation. The only thing the parents really had control over was how packed the week was when they returned. This was not the week to schedule a night out with girlfriends or to host an event at their home! If the parents could have somehow lowered their own stress level for those first few days back (not easy, I know), it would have been an easier week, although still not easy. But mental preparation is half the battle. Know it will be tough, but vacations are worth it. You'll remember the wonderful trip for much longer than you'll remember the tough few days that followed it.

Finally, know *your* child and make flexibility decisions accordingly. There are some children who can go with their parents to a dinner party on Friday or Saturday night, stay up until ten, sleep in the next morning, and still be right on track for bedtime the next day. There are other children who, if they lose even one hour of their usual sleep routine, will be a disaster the next day. The parents then must weigh the importance of the occasion with the temperament of the child. Perhaps for a wedding, it's worth keeping the child up. For a dinner out with another family, however, perhaps it's not. You also need to be prepared for meltdowns, and know when

> EMMA TIP
>
> Don't be so wedded to schedules that you are unwilling to listen to your child. If your child's hungry half an hour early, you should feed her; it's not a big deal. Use schedules as rules of thumb, but not to the extreme.

to make haste for the nearest exit. If you're pushing the envelope, then have a plan. Warn your hosts ahead of time, order the food the moment you get into the restaurant, and take two cars, just in case.

> **PARENT TIP**
>
> If we have dinner at a friend's house, we have our bath and change into pajamas there, to stick to our routine and make it easy to get to bed as soon as we get home.

☑ Are you okay with your child getting dirty, exploring, and running free (within reason)?

I'm very particular and somewhat of a perfectionist (who am I kidding? I'm a perfectionist through and through). Once when my mum came to visit, as soon as she put a glass down, whether she'd finished with it or not, I put it in the dishwasher. I like things the way I like them, and I feel an affinity with parents who think the same way. But that's what's so wonderful about kids. Over the years, working with them has taught me to let a lot of stuff go, and I'm better off for it. So what if a glass is sitting out? It's just not important.

We are so often telling our kids what they can't do—what about shifting to what they *can* do? No, you don't want that loud toy in the kitchen, but they can and should be able to take it outside. **Let kids be kids.** It may seem obvious, but I have to remind parents constantly. I say to mums (who have temperaments like mine) all the time, "Let it go—who cares if they get dirty or make a mess? We'll clean it up and they'll help." If you're working on such a tight schedule that you have no time for cleanup, then that's a sign your schedule is too busy. Don't be too busy to allow your kids the freedom to be kids. And teaching them there's a time to be messy and a time to be clean is incredibly valuable.

DIY Schedule

The best way to bring everything in this chapter together, of course, is by making your own schedule. Below I've included several sample schedules for different age groups and circumstances. These are not meant to be followed to the letter, but rather to give a sense of what a day should look like. Use them as guides, but make a schedule that fits your life, and your child's.

SIX-MONTH-OLD

6:00–7:00 a.m.: awake

7:00–7:15: milk, and then solids

8:00–9:30: playtime at home

9:30/10:00–11:30: first nap

11:30: milk

12:00 p.m.: solids

12:30–2:00: out of the house—errands with adult, walks, playtime

2:00–3:30/4:00: second nap

3:30/4:00: milk

4:00–5:30: play on floor, read books with parent, fresh air

5:30: solids

5:45–6:45: playtime—peekaboo, soft blocks, etc.

6:45: bath

7:00: milk/bedtime

TWO-YEAR-OLD WHO STAYS HOME

7:00 a.m.: awake

7:30–8:00: breakfast and getting ready for day

9:00: walk to the park; play

10:00: snack

10:00–11:00: art project, reading with parent

11:00–11:30: independent playtime (This is a time when your child is encouraged to use his imagination and play freely on his own.)

11:30: lunchtime

12:00–2:00 p.m.: stories and naptime

2:00: snack

2:30–4:00: outing with adult—errands, library, or playdate

4:00–5:00: playtime at home—some with parent, some alone

5:00–5:30: dinner

5:30–6:30: playtime at home—some with parent, some alone

6:30–7:00: cleanup and getting ready to go for a bath

7:00–7:30: bath, jammies, book, and bed

FOUR-YEAR-OLD WHO GOES TO DAYCARE

7:00 a.m.: wakes up, gets dressed, feeds the dog

7:30: has breakfast

7:45: brushes teeth, puts on shoes

8:00: leaves for school

8:30 a.m.–5:00 p.m.: school (1.5 hours quiet time during daycare, plus exercise time, focus time, and two snack times)

5:00–6:00: helps Mum prepare dinner (quality time) and eats dinner; clears table

6:00–6:45: free-play time—dressing up; coloring; playing with Barbies, cars, Lego, etc.

6:45–7:00: cleans up and gets ready for a bath

7:00–7:30: bath, jammies, book

7:30–7:45: looks at books quietly in bed by herself before lights out

SIX-YEAR-OLD WHO GOES TO FIRST GRADE

7:00 a.m.: wakes up, gets dressed, makes bed

7:30: feeds dog, gets schoolbag ready, eats breakfast

8:00–8:30: free time

9:00 a.m.–3:30 p.m.: school (school includes exercise time, focused time, and lunchtime)

3:30: snack at home, then outdoor playtime

4:00*–4:45: homework

4:45–5:30: free time

5:30: sets table, eats dinner with family

6:15–7:00: quality time with parents—board game, basketball, family time

7:00–7:15: cleanup

7:15–8:00: wind-down time—bath, pajamas, books, bed

---

* 4:00–7:00: After-school activities (swimming, soccer, language and music classes) may fall in this window once or twice a week.

CHAPTER SEVEN

The Maginot Line

Boundaries and Consequences

"Trade in the sling for a slingshot and think about the kid you want to shoot out into the world when you're no longer there."

—Nicola Kraus, The Huffington Post

CHECKLIST

- ☑ Does your child hear and understand "no"?
- ☑ Is your child clear about what his consequences will be?
- ☑ Is your child given the chance to correct his behavior?
- ☑ Are you firm? Do you follow through?
- ☑ Are you making a tantrum your *child's* problem, not yours?
- ☑ Do you maintain a poker face when your child experiences a consequence?
- ☑ Are you willing to let your child be upset?

☑ Are you willing to let your child experience healthy fear?

☑ Are you supportive of teachers' and others' efforts to set boundaries and enforce consequences with your child?

☑ Are the boundaries consistent?

☑ Are *you* consistent?

☑ Do you trust your child to adhere to nonphysical boundaries?

☑ Do you let your child pick herself up when she falls?

☑ Do you hold your child accountable for her actions?

☑ Do you avoid arguing and negotiating?

☑ Are you letting your child make his own choices?

☑ Do you resist offering bribes?

☑ Are you picking your battles?

LET'S DISCUSS SHOES for a moment, shall we?

Here is a common scene: Mum is trying to get her school-aged daughter ready for a trip to the park. It is forty degrees outside and yet the daughter wants to wear sandals. What does Mum do? Does she

a. tell her daughter no, sandals are not appropriate for the weather, and steel herself for the ensuing battle;

b. tell her daughter fine, but sneak a warm pair of wellies and some socks in the backpack for when her daughter realizes she's misjudged the situation;

c. let her daughter make the choice, but advise her that it is cold, she will probably be uncomfortable with sandals, and that they are not returning home for new shoes should that be the case?

How you answer this question relies in large part on where and how you were brought up, how your peers would handle the situation, and a myriad of other cultural influences. Most parents I know would choose a or b. I would choose c. American parents tend to want to control their children's choices (as in answer a), or to bail them out so they don't have to suffer consequences (as in answer b). As long as frostbite isn't a possibility (in which case it would be a safety issue and worthy of the perennial parental trump card), I see no problem with letting the daughter wear the shoes she wants to and letting her be cold. She will likely make a better choice the next time. Chilly toes are a reasonable price to pay for a lesson about making autonomous choices.

I have a Scottish friend, Susan, who works in Chicago as a nanny for several young children. When she takes the kids to school, most parents cut across the parking lot with their children. Not Susan. She parks in the same lot as everyone else, but then walks the kids on the sidewalk around the perimeter of the parking lot. It takes twice as long to reach the school entrance, but Susan is teaching the children an important lesson about boundaries, traffic safety, and rules. Doing otherwise sends the wrong message to your kids that it's okay to cut corners, even if it's a parking lot.

In contrast, let's look again at the toddler triplets I've mentioned. Their crazy busy, sleep-deprived parents added to their chaos by constantly stepping over the countless baby gates they'd erected. There were gates around the entertainment center, gates around the kitchen cabinets, gates around everything grown-up that they didn't want their children to touch. Instead of teaching their children boundaries and rules about what they could and couldn't touch, and then enforcing those rules, they put up walls everywhere.

I love putting these stories next to each other because they show two completely different ways of looking at the issue of boundaries. A British parent is much more likely to let her child wear sandals on a cold day. A British parent is much more likely to allow her child to find her own way home at a young age. Would you allow your nine-year-old to take the subway in New York City on his own? American mum and writer Lenore Skenazy did and was heavily criticized, dubbed by the media as "the world's worst mom." In England parents let their kids do this at an early age. Maybe not nine, but certainly there are ten- and eleven-year-olds riding the Tube alone.

Why not let kids be outside without you, provided you're within earshot and the backyard is safe? Why not trust them to come and get you if there's a problem, and sit and enjoy a cup of tea in the meanwhile?

The baby gate fortress, the scenario with the mum not wanting her daughter to wear sandals, and the criticism of Skenazy as "the world's worst mom" have one thing in common: overprotectiveness. This is a problem with American parenting. Parents put so much pressure on themselves and try to control far too much. We see other caregivers walking their children by the hand everywhere, and we think we must, too, lest we be accused of being careless or less loving. Part of it may also be that we are used to controlling other parts of our lives. We know how long a movie will last to the minute, as well as precisely how long it will take to get to the theater using a particular route; we are accustomed to ringing or texting and getting ahold of anyone we want at almost any time. Often, our lives are so busy that we need (or think we need) this control and precision. It's no wonder that we apply the same force to our child rearing.

There is another root as well, something we've already touched on: many American parents feel that *more* is better, whether it involves supersizing their soft drink, buying the latest iPhone, or overprotecting their children. They believe that their child should always be near them; they should always respond instantaneously when their child calls. We know we have a tendency to overdo it, too, which is why David Vienna's blog post about his new parenting trend—known as "CTFD" or "Calm the F*** Down" went viral. We don't need to stand guard over our children, but we do need to teach them, and then trust them. It does not mean we are too neglectful if we allow them to explore on their own. Doing *less* is about relinquishing a bit of control—that's a good thing for them, and it's a good thing for us.

The difficulty with giving up control applies not only to setting boundaries, but also to consequences. Frequently I see parents engaging with their child's tantrums and trying to bring that child back around through force of will. "Stop crying," they say. "Stop crying now and apologize so we can move on!" Communicating with a child while she's in the midst of a tantrum only feeds it. Really what these parents need to do is give the child space to cool off and *let the child come to them*, explaining "You can join us as soon as you calm down and you're ready to play nicely." **But it will only work if you then *let go*.** If the child misses out on dessert or family playtime, that's his choice and he must bear the consequence, just as the grade-schooler must experience the cold toes to learn not to wear sandals on a cold day. The parent cannot coerce her into making the right choice at every moment, but must take a step back and let the child experience the consequences.

☑ Does your child hear and understand "no"?

The word "no" has a bad rap. There are experts who will tell you that it limits your child's self-expression and creativity, that it's a bad word, that it's not even effective. You absolutely *must* use the word "no" sometimes. "No" is a powerful tool, and it's high time American parents reclaimed it. It's best paired with a concise, simple explanation, like "No, you mustn't hit your brother, because that hurts his body," as we discussed in Chapter Two, "The King's Speech," on communication. However, don't get caught up in justifying rules to your child. I only explain once, or twice at the most. After that, if the behavior continues, I say a simple but firm "no" and move them away from whatever it is.

Your children will hear "no" again and again when they enter the real world; it is your job as the parent to teach them how to cope with hearing it.

☑ Is your child clear about what his consequences will be?

Just as it's critical for children to fully understand the behaviors expected of them, as we covered in Chapter Two, it's critical for them to understand the specific consequences if they do not comply. So often I visit families who are missing this piece. If a child balks at being told to clean up Play-Doh, a parent might say, "I told you to

EMMA TIP

Here are three suggestions for making "no" effective:

1. Don't overuse it, because your children will tune you out if they hear it too many times.
2. Explain, briefly, why you are saying it. If they are reaching for the oven, for instance, say, "No. The oven is hot, it could hurt you."
3. Make sure your body language and tone convey that you mean what you say. Get on their level, hold their arms (not roughly), look in their eyes, and speak confidently.

EMMA TIP

Always try to tie consequences to the action happening *at the moment*. A few examples:

Child misbehaving at home before a birthday party = "If you don't stop this behavior right now, you will *not* go to the party. You'll stay home and do nothing."

Child misbehaving at a playdate = "We're at a playdate and you need to find your manners and play nicely. If you can't, then we're going home. This is your last warning. Once more and we're going home."

Child throwing a book = "If you throw that again, you are going to lose the book."

Child throwing food at dinner = "If you throw food again, I will take it away and you'll have nothing else to eat."

Keep the consequence immediate.

please clean it up and come inside. Now I'm going to count to three. That's one! That's two!" But the child doesn't know what will happen next, and so doesn't comply. The child needs to be told what will happen. "I told you to please clean it up and come inside. I'm going to count to three and if you don't clean it up, I'm taking it away for the rest of the day." Clear, specific. I think the reason parents often don't add this last part is that, well, sometimes it's hard to think about what a consequence will be! Particularly if you're in a public setting or if your attention is divided.

Whatever you do, don't make threats you know are empty. I constantly hear parents say, "If you don't stop that tantrum, I'm going to leave you behind." The child knows full well the parent isn't going to leave him, and I can almost hear the child, by virtue of his expression, saying, "Yeah, right!" All these empty threats do is devalue you and your word. I'm certainly not suggesting that you leave your child behind, only that you say what you can follow through with, and what you're *prepared* to follow through with.

There are also some consequences that should be off-limits. You don't want to withhold the bedtime routine, your love, their special blanket, or givens like school. Again, it may sound obvious, but many the exasperated parent has said, "If you don't cooperate and get your pajamas on now, I'll take away your lovey," or ". . . there will be no snuggling tonight." Instead, say, "If you don't hurry up and get you're PJs on, we'll only have time for one book instead of two." You're not giving them a threat; you're offering them a *choice*.

☑ Is your child given the chance to correct his behavior?

Once I observed a five-year-old boy roughhousing too hard with his little brother. His father swooped in and sent the older boy to his room. The boy wasn't given the chance to change his behavior. The next time he acted out, he similarly was not given the chance to course-correct, and his behavior grew even *worse*. When the family was in a setting where they couldn't easily remove him, he was incapable of responding to his parents' requests. Giving children the chance to change their behavior on the spot serves as an important lesson about boundaries and consequences. It also teaches

PARENT TIP

I used to suggest consequences that would be way too difficult for me to follow through with, but now before explaining a consequence to my son, I think through how I'll feel carrying it out and make sure I buy into it fully. Just taking a moment to do this makes a difference in how confident I am when I explain it to him. It's almost like he could sense the uncertainty in my voice when I'd say something like "You are not going to get television privileges tonight if you continue whining . . ." (knowing as I did that I needed him to be occupied with the TV so I could get dinner on the table!).

EMMA TIP

"Counting," or giving your child to the count of three, is a popular technique applied when helping a child correct his behavior. Though I don't often use counting methods myself, I think they can be very effective, with two caveats. First, a parent shouldn't allow too long for the child to change his behavior. Counting to five is too much—the child will want to stretch it out. Second, do not indulge in the "three and a half . . ." measurement. It teaches children that the method is negotiable. Soon they will turn it into "three and three-quarters . . ." and before you know it, you will be counting to the equivalent of twenty in order to get a simple task completed or a negative behavior stopped. I understand how tempting it is, however! You are sitting at a crossroads, where your son is SO CLOSE to complying and you can get on with it and go to the park if you give him more time, or you can sit and wait while he has a temper tantrum. That is why "two" morphs to "two-and-a-half" so easily! Stay strong. Perhaps you'll get to the park more quickly today if you stretch out the counting, but over time you will spend so much more time counting and coercing.

self-control, a huge and invaluable life lesson. And believe it or not, it leads to less frustration for them, and thus less of a fight for you.

"Frustration" is the critical word here; being a kid is frustrating. Sometimes kids react on impulse—they'll throw a block because they didn't really think it through beforehand. Let them know that it wasn't okay to throw the block because it could have hurt someone, and that if they throw the block again, the blocks will be taken away. Then it's his choice whether he gets to keep playing with the blocks or not. Can you imagine if you did something pretty minor at work, but your manager swooped in and gave you a written warning versus coming to you and asking you to do it differently? You'd be furious. Children who are punished without warning feel the same way.

Do note, however, that some behaviors absolutely warrant immediate action. Kicking, hitting, or biting do not justify warnings.

From a very young age children should know these behaviors are wrong, and removing them from a situation immediately is fair and expresses the severity of their mistake. In one family I've worked with, when a two-year-old boy tried to throw a heavy pumpkin on his four-month-old brother, I took him aside immediately, got down to his level, held both arms, and raised my voice in a firm tone. "You must not throw anything at your brother," I told him. "Pumpkins are not for throwing. You could really hurt him and now you can't play with it anymore. Go pick up the pumpkin and apologize to your brother right now." The boy cried for a while but we talked about his feelings afterward and an hour later he was laughing and playing again—this time not so dangerously.

☑ Are you firm? Do you follow through?

I was once asked to observe a family's interactions around boundaries, and noted the following transaction:

MUM: We're leaving now.
CHILD: Nooooooo!
MUM: I'm going to count to three, and then I'll have to carry you.
ME (THINKING): *Good job, mum!*
MUM: One . . . Two . . .
CHILD: Nooooo! I don't want to leave!
MUM: Three! Do you want to walk or can I carry you?
ME: (thinking) *Oh dear . . . she's just lost all her power.*

Their exchange went on for what seemed like forever! And then the same thing happened when she was trying to get the child into the car seat.

Lack of firmness and follow-through is the number one problem

I see when it comes to boundaries and consequences. And it is all too easy to understand why. So many of the parents I know work incredibly hard, whether it's out of the home or not. Two mums for whom I have nothing but compassion come to mind.

Nadia was a single working mum with two young boys who had worked her into a state of perpetual exhaustion. Their dad was not particularly helpful, financially or otherwise, and Nadia had a great deal of stress on her shoulders. All day long she tried to set boundaries with the boys: no screaming; eat your food before you can be excused; stop hitting your brother. She said she was going to put them in their rooms if they didn't comply, and she would even count to three with the understanding that once she hit three, that was it. But then, nothing. No follow-through. Nadia simply didn't have the energy to follow through with the punishments she threatened, when (1) *keeping* them in their room represented another battle she'd have to fight, and (2) as soon as that punishment was carried through, another would inevitably follow. There were just too many broken rules, and she didn't want to be prison guard all day.

Sophia's problem was similar. She had two daughters, and though her husband was at home, he often wasn't engaged and left most of the parenting to her. Sophia worked all day, and then took the majority of the responsibility for the girls each night. She was tired and especially worn down when it came to putting the girls to bed. As if her daughters could sense this, they fought at bedtime. Straightaway, they said they were hungry and wanted a snack, but Sophia said no. An hour and a half later, after countless sojourns out of their bedroom, whining, crying, and screaming, Sophia had had it. Her own bed was calling to her loudly. She was at her limit. "Fine!" she said. "I'll get you some cereal and *then* you are going to bed!" Kids: 2, Parents: 0

What caregiver *can't* relate to Sophia or Nadia? We've all been there, and know all too well the feelings of desperation: I'll do anything to get some peace! My job in these cases is to remind parents of the bigger picture. Yes, of course giving in on the boys' punishment will mean less crying this afternoon. Yes, of course giving the girls the cereal will get you to bed earlier tonight. But what about tomorrow night? What about the night after? What about five years from now, when they want to go to a party and don't feel like coming home? As children get older, the "problems" get bigger and if you can't control them now, you're in for a world of trouble.

What's more, children really want you to set firm limits with them. It's disconcerting for them to have free reign, or for them to feel unclear about who's in charge. They may not want to stop playing at the moment you're asking them to, and thus their appreciation for limits is hard to see, but they *do* want them.

Remaining firm and following through is probably the single biggest difference a parent can make. I make no claims that it won't be painful at first, and parents should be prepared. But it will work, and it won't take long. When children realize that you will do what you say, and you will do so again and again, they will accept your rules, and they will have more respect for you. **Caving in might be easier in the short term, but much harder in the long run.**

> **EMMA TIP**
>
> Always balance being firm with being loving. That doesn't mean you cuddle right after you've disciplined, but it does mean that you should have many moments that are loving and affectionate. As you'll see in the next chapter, I'm not a fan of British households that are all rules and limits and no love. I'm also not a fan of American households that are so loving of their kids that the kids can do no wrong. There's a balance.

☑ Are you making a tantrum your *child's* problem, not yours?

If your child is whining or having a tantrum, she is probably doing it for your benefit. **Children will seek attention, whether it be neg-**

ative or positive. Tell her that if she wants to whine, that's fine, but (if you're at home) send her to another room, or you leave the room you're in. The main point: don't try to reason with a tantruming child. At the same time, you can acknowledge her by saying, "I will be right here when you've calmed down and are ready to talk about it." This response has three wonderful benefits:

1. It gives her a choice.
2. It takes the *attention* away from the attention-getting behavior.
3. It's a great coping mechanism for parents. It means that you don't have to listen to whining!

☑ *Do you maintain a poker face when your child experiences a consequence?*

Let's assume your child has a tantrum during a family reunion at a restaurant. Following through on a consequence you'd explained beforehand, you leave the reunion with your child and sit in the parked car. If you have to sit in a car with a screaming child instead of catching up with your relatives over a nice meal, obviously that affects you. But you must act as if you don't mind a whit. The more upset you show you are, the more the child will want to engage with you about it. Instead, check your phone. Read the car owner's manual. Act as if the wait is not a big deal to you. Do not talk or interact with your child until he tells you he is ready to go back to the reunion and behave nicely. Children do not like to be bored, and it's boring for them if they can't argue with you as well as if their behavior isn't getting any attention. They will eventually come around and comply.

Kids sense when you're irritated or weak, and if there's a chance they may be able to push your buttons and get away with

something or just get a reaction out of you, they will. The calmer you are, the better your message will be delivered. That said, it isn't easy! Just recently I lapsed in this department, and I am *always* calm. I was really tired and a two-year-old I was caring for was spiraling out of control. The first reason was that he hadn't napped, and the second reason was that I wasn't as calm as I could've been. My poker face weakened; he knew his behavior was getting to me, and so he did it all the more. Had I just followed my advice from the previous discussion and put him in another room away from his brother and me, I would have remained calm and he could have behaved however he wanted without it bothering me.

☑ Are you willing to let your child be upset?

Here's a familiar scenario: You're at a toy store with your child picking up a gift for a birthday party. Your child sees a doll she really wants and asks you if she can have it. Do you

a. tell her "No, we're not getting a toy today. We're buying a toy for your friend's birthday";

b. buy it for her because it's unrealistic for her to walk out empty-handed;

c. say not today, but she can put it on her birthday list, or save up to buy it herself?

Your answer can actually be a or c. Answer a is perfectly adequate, and my top choice, but sometimes you may not want to close off completely the possibility of the toy, especially as it could be a good opportunity to promote earning and saving. If the child has a special day coming up, tell her to make a list that you can share with relatives. But so many parents answer b because they either don't want to deal with a meltdown or they don't want their child to feel upset. Some parents put it on themselves, thinking it wasn't fair of them to put their child in such a situation of temptation (like bringing a child to a candy store and not allowing him candy). **Little do they recognize it's not unfair, but it's actually a wonderful opportunity to teach their child a valuable lesson: They do not get everything they want or ask for.**

☑ Are you willing to let your child experience healthy fear?

Parents just need to be the parents and not their child's friend. They need to stop fearing their kids, and their kids should experience a healthy amount of fear themselves! Not necessarily of their *parents*, but of the consequences of their actions. Without fear of consequences, what's to stop that child from driving under the influence when he's older? Or doing other illegal or dangerous things? Consequences do require some fear, and parents need to stop protecting their children from it. Healthy fear will keep them safe and help them make good choices independently.

> **EMMA TIP**
>
> I have a "look" I use with children I take care of, and when they see that expression on my face, no words are necessary. They understand they've crossed the line, and they immediately pull it together for fear of the consequences. Having a look that your children recognize and associate with a breach of behavior is indispensable for moments when you can't use words.

☑ Are you supportive of teachers' and others' efforts to set boundaries and enforce consequences with your child?

Carrie, a wonderful woman I used to nanny for, teaches dance lessons for kids. Recently she had a student who was so obnoxious and distracting to the other dancers that Carrie asked her to leave the studio. It wasn't long before the girl's dad came storming in and pitched a fit. "Excuse me," Carrie said calmly, "but I won't let my own kids be disrespectful toward me, and I won't let your daughter be disrespectful to me or to the other students." Carrie's strength on the matter is unfortunately a rarity. When parents attack teachers as this dad did Carrie, teachers tend to back down.

There are two problems here. The first: *Why are the parents attacking the teachers?* I'm not saying teachers are always 100 percent right, but they are in a position of authority when they're at the head of a classroom, and children need to respect that. Why would the children respect the teacher's authority if the parent doesn't? A good friend of mine who is a headmaster in England is mortified when he observes this dynamic in American schools. In England, if children get into trouble at school, they are incredibly distraught because they know that when their parents find out about it, their punishment will worsen. In the United States, a child's response to his teacher's discipline efforts is more likely to be "Wait until I tell my mum and dad what that horrible teacher did to me!" The parents, unable to admit their child is wrong, or perhaps just embarrassed their child is less than perfect, go on the attack.

The second problem: *Why are the teachers backing down?* That's easier to answer and inextricably linked to the first problem. They often *have* to back down, because they don't have the power they once had. Parents rule the schools, and students rule the parents. The teachers are stuck in an impossible situation, as it's become a matter of culture as much as anything else. We *must* get back to the place where children can be held accountable by the grown-ups around them, even if the grown-ups are not their parent.

☑ Are the boundaries consistent?

Boundaries should not be bounded by walls. If so, it creates an underlying confusion for children, and chances are, the boundaries you were once successful in setting up at home will deteriorate. Rules should be the same for home and for the world at large. While of course there are certain exceptions—ball throwing is fine outside, naturally, but not so in the living room—it is important to be clear and consistent when it comes to rules, and not to complicate matters by having a separate set of expectations.

Parents often expect their children to understand the difference between public and private spaces, and to know that it's not okay to do underarm farting noises at a restaurant even though you let them do it at home. After all, *we* say things at home to our spouses or on the phone to our friends that we wouldn't dream of saying at work. *We* goof around and let loose at home in ways we don't when we're at restaurants. We assume our kids are capable of these same distinctions, and to some extent they are (e.g., it's okay to get undressed in front of Mummy in the bathroom, but not to lift your dress in public). But it is difficult for kids to shift from one set of rules to another all the time, and they should not be expected to. It's confusing and it won't work.

Or perhaps the parent is careful about *enforcing* rules at home, but not in public. Perhaps Mum or Dad doesn't want to create a scene in public, and so gives in to the child's wishes. This is a lot more harmful than it seems. Children are smart. They will see the holes in the fence and make them larger and larger. They will learn to reserve their demands for public settings when they know Mum or Dad is likely to give in. Children will say otherwise, but they want those boundaries and they want that consistency. It gives them a sense of safety and security to know boundaries are there. I believe their underlying need for consistent boundaries is a large part of why it is possible to improve a child's behavior so quickly. They follow along because they *want* to.

☑ Are *you* consistent?

If I have a temper tantrum in Prada because I want an expensive handbag for free, I will probably be removed from the premises and possibly arrested. I know this, of course, which is why I don't do it. But what if I pitched a fit in Prada and the manager took pity on me and gave me a bag? I would have learned that crying and carrying on is an effective way to achieve my objective. Or what if I tantrumed there for five different days, and on the fifth day, I finally got my way? I would have learned that managers are inconsistent; therefore, I should always tantrum just in case it's a day when I'll get lucky and get a free bag. And trust me, if this were the case, I'd be having some serious daily tantrums in Prada!

If staying consistent and firm is commonsense advice, it is just as true that it is incredibly hard to follow. I once coached a mum who was having a devil of a time getting her three kids under control. We spent several days together, working on the techniques in this checklist, and slowly but surely, the kids were coming around. They listened when their mum told them to do something; they knew she would follow through with a specific consequence if they misbehaved. Then came a test: We visited a grocery store. One of the children pitched a noisy, embarrassing fit the entire time because she wanted to sit in the cart, which was far too dangerous. Mum had three options:

a. She could give in to her and thus reinforce the child's behavior.

b. She could load everyone back into the car immediately and thus neglect to get the groceries she needed for the night (and if the tantruming child's objective was to leave, this is another form of giving in).

c. She could withstand the glares and stares of her fellow shoppers as her daughter screamed down every aisle.

Which would you do? None of these options is particularly appealing, right? And yet there is a correct answer: c. Withstanding the glares of fellow shoppers is undoubtedly painful, which is why consistency is so difficult. But in all likelihood, that scene will not be repeated, and if it is, it won't last for as long. And if Mum gave in to the child, all the ground she'd gained with her kids at home would be lost. That child needed to get the message that Mum was going to do her shopping whether she had a tantrum or not. Mum has certain standards of behavior she expects, *always*. The next time Mum takes her to the store, Mum must do the same thing. If she gives in and lets her daughter sit in the cart, then all of the embarrassment they experienced on the previous trip was for nothing—it's just like the temper tantrum in Prada. It's worth five temper tantrums to get one free Prada purse, believe me! And if Dad or Grandma takes her to the store, they mustn't allow her to sit in the cart, either.

Consistency is such a large and critical piece of boundaries and consequences, and that's another reason why communicating with other caregivers is critical. As we covered in Chapter Two, I suggest that parents sit together and discuss their child's problem behaviors and their expectations. What is acceptable and what is not? They might even make a list, and then look together at that list. Mum and Dad should agree on the areas of focus, and commit to working on them with their child, then be consistent about how they will do so.

☑ **Do you trust your child to adhere to nonphysical boundaries?**

In the case of the triplets, I convinced the parents to remove the gates that had turned their comfortable home into a fortress. Sure enough, the children went directly to the expensive entertainment center and tried to touch it. "No," we explained, "that's not for you to touch." We turned them around to face away from the equipment and gave them something they were allowed to play with. They returned to the entertainment center several times, and we repeated telling them "no" several times. That was it. They understood that they were not allowed to play with the entertainment center, and if they tried, they would be removed. Sometimes this kind of boundary setting will spark a tantrum at first, and that's okay. Remove the child to a safe place and allow him to calm down. But keep firm on your boundary.

I also recognize that sometimes setting a nonphysical boundary takes more energy to enforce. A parent may have to be hypervigilant for a time to make sure that the off-limits area is not returned to in a moment of curiosity or when a parental back is turned. Remember the family from Chapter Two whose daughter kept running from their side street to the road? It would have given the parents more assurance, I'm sure, to have built a ten-foot-tall fence all around the home's perimeter, and a fence would have required less vigilance. But they had no control of their daughter and needed to establish some. They couldn't put up fences everywhere, after all. So instead, they taught her what her boundaries were, and she faced consequences if she did not adhere to them.

Above all, keep firm. It is well worth the time investment. Once the child sees that you are serious, he will stop fighting the boundary. It takes much less time than you think, and reaps all sorts of rewards: not just the removal of a baby gate, for example, but also the child's grasp on self-restraint. He must understand that he does not have full reign over the domain.

☑ Do you let your child pick herself up when she falls?

With younger children, this question of picking themselves up is literal. Many toddlers fall quite a bit when they are learning to walk and run. I always look to see what happens in this common occurrence. If a child is hurt, go to him, absolutely and always. But again, it's not uncommon for an eighteen-month-old to fall repeatedly from a standing position, and as children that age are not very far from the ground, it's unlikely a fall in the middle of a room is cause for physical harm. Still, the parental reaction when this happens is very telling. If Mum or Dad races to the child at the first stumble, that is what the child comes to expect. Why stand up on her own when a cry will bring Mum or Dad running and picking her up? It's so much more pleasant and takes less effort when someone else puts you back on your feet. And yet, what kind of a lesson does that teach?

☑ Do you hold your child accountable for her actions?

With older children, the stumbles may not be physical, but they still exist. If a seven-year-old repeatedly leaves her homework at home,

PARENT TIP

When my first child was about fifteen months old, she would constantly throw her bottle of milk onto the floor from her high chair, and then cry for me to pick it up. Mealtimes were a constant process of me bending down to pick up the bottle. When a visiting friend who had older children saw this routine, she told my daughter sternly and calmly that if she dropped the bottle again, it would be taken away. And amazingly, the "game" stopped. I hadn't realized my toddler was capable of understanding and responding to a consequence like that, and it changed my entire approach to setting boundaries with her!

and each time you bring it to school for her, then she is not learning accountability. Why would she remember it if you're always coming to her rescue? Instead, let her know if she forgets her homework again, you will not bring it to her—and then *don't*. Let her receive a penalty from her teacher instead. The more parents remove their child's consequences, the less the child grasps that negative consequences exist, and the less responsible they'll be.

☑ Do you avoid arguing and negotiating?

Most children want to have the last word. "But I really, really want to watch a movie, Mummy! I've been so good today. I'll watch something educational. Terry gets to watch movies every day." Let them talk all they want. If they can't get you angry and push your buttons, their attempts to engage you in an argument will end very quickly, as they'll get bored. Explain your reasoning once, then move on. They may act like a stuck record, but that doesn't mean you need to go in circles with them. You are not a diplomat, and you don't need to negotiate or get into long conversations about why your child is feeling a certain way. **Sometimes an answer is just plain "no" and it's time to move on.**

☑ Are you letting your child make his own choices?

The Miller family had a problem one morning. The family had gone out to dinner the previous night, and the eight-year-old son, Trevor, hadn't finished his dessert but had wrapped it up to have another time. Now he wanted it for breakfast. He refused to eat anything other than the leftover dessert for breakfast, and looked as if he was on the verge of pitching a fit. Everyone needed to leave for school and work, and Trevor looked ready to hijack the peaceful morning.

The best course of action for Mum and Dad is to let Trevor make a choice. "Trevor, you can have your dessert when you get home from school or I can throw it in the garbage right now. Which would you like to do?" If he chooses to have a hunger strike for the morning, vowing not to eat any breakfast if he can't have his dessert, let him. If he chooses not to eat, he chooses not to eat. He'll be hungry, but he will get over it. And the next day he'll know you will follow through, and that he will experience the consequences.

The point here is that the choice should be Trevor's. **Choices empower kids, and more than almost anything else, they want to feel a sense of control over their lives.** Of course, ultimately you as the parent have the control: you are deciding the options they have. But then you must be okay with whatever they choose. If you have to throw away the dessert, so be it. So many parents want to help guide the choice so the child doesn't suffer the consequence, but that's entirely detrimental to everyone!

EMMA TIP

Choices are particularly important when it comes to the battleground of the closet— particularly for little girls. Give her two choices for outfits—no more, or else she might be overwhelmed—and let her choose which outfit to wear. If she still has trouble deciding, say, "If you can't choose, then Mummy or Daddy will choose for you." She'll soon realize that if she wants to choose her outfit, she'd better hurry up and choose one of the outfits you picked.

☑ *Do you resist offering bribes?*

A common bad habit: giving your child something every time she does something that should be expected of her as a civilized human being. I once observed a mum, Stacey, who couldn't get the slightest amount of cooperation from her children without promising them

EMMA TIP

Parents frequently ask me where I fall on the subject of giving an allowance. If a child is older— perhaps around eight—and you're trying to teach him how to handle his money, then it's appropriate to give him money for doing extra chores around the house. But there are some tasks that should just be expected, like keeping his room tidy, sitting nicely at the table, making his bed, and feeding the dog. If, however, he picks up the dog poop in the backyard, then that seems like a rewardable effort. Allowance is also a great way to help you say "yes" when there's a toy your child wants. If you're at the store and he sees a Buzz Lightyear he must have, you can say, "That's great—you can do some extra chores around the house and once you've earned enough, I'll bring you back here and you can buy it."

something in return. She bribed them to get into the car. She negotiated with them about where to sit. Exhausting! She needed to just say, "You need to get into the car. If you don't, I'm going to help your body do it." Most behaviors should just be expected, not rewarded with a sticker or promise of a treat or something. It's important to acknowledge good behavior, to say, for example, "Thank you for waiting so patiently," but acknowledging is far different from offering a reward for waiting patiently.

☑ Are you picking your battles?

As we saw from Nadia, sometimes it's just too exhausting to play rule-enforcer. She was setting both herself and her children up for failure by trying to correct all of their behavior all of the time. Everyone wants and needs to have fun and connection free of reprimands. If it's a particularly trying time, or if your child seems to relish testing, *pick your battles*. For instance, one mum I know was raising a very strong-willed daughter who was almost three. One morning was full of Mum's pleas and reprimands: "Drink all of your juice—no, don't drink it there; use two hands; sit on the potty right now; stop running from me; pick up your toys before we go . . ." and on and on. They decided to go to the park, and Mum started struggling with her daughter to put on her sweatshirt. The little girl had had enough, and was screaming and running and was dead-set against putting on that sweatshirt. In that case, Mum could just let it go. It wasn't that cold outside, and even if it was, children cannot actually get sick from being too cold (unless it's cold enough for them to get hypothermia). Since it wasn't an issue of health or safety, the worst-case scenario was that her daughter would be cold. In a morning full of battles, this one was not worth fighting.

I'm not suggesting that you give in. And in fact, in this case of the mum and the sweatshirt, she could find a happy compromise, such as asking her daughter to please carry her sweatshirt if she wasn't going to wear it. Sometimes the best course of action is to make fewer rules but to enforce the rules you have.

> EMMA TIP
>
> A great way to gauge whether the battle is worth it or not is to ask yourself, *What are the consequences of sitting this one out?* If it's a safety issue or a respect issue, it's worth fighting. But if it's a cosmetic one, or something more minor, the best course will be to let it go.

Supporting the Sapling

I like to think of a tree sapling when it comes to the issue of boundaries and consequences. A sapling requires support and guidance in the form of a stake and tree tie. During the tree's initial growth, it is essential that it have this support to ensure its establishment. As the sapling grows into a tree, the tie is loosened periodically and slowly, allowing it to support itself until such a time that the stake and tie can be removed altogether, encouraging the tree to flourish and grow on its own path. There are times that the tie could have been loosened too early and the tree may begin to grow in the wrong direction/angle; in this instance, simply tighten the tie again to get it back on track. But you mustn't neglect to loosen the tie. One of the most common parenting mistakes I see is the inability to loosen the tie, to loosen the "leash," and to let children experience consequences.

I've said it before and will say it again. When it comes to boundaries and consequences, if you do the work up front, there will be a payoff. But you must do the work. I wish I could sit with every tired parent and reassure him or her that the payoff will come. I wish I could enter every stressed-out home personally to cheerlead and help parents be firmer and more consistent. But since I can't, take my written assurance: It will get easier. It will make a difference. It is hard, but also easier than you think. In that way, it's much like dieting. Every so often a newfangled dieting approach or pill comes along and dieters rejoice that there is a breakthrough! Only to find out, the solution is actually pretty simple: burn more calories than you consume, and you will lose weight. The same is true of boundaries and consequences: they are hard, you will want to weaken your resolve, you will want to be less than consistent, you will want a magic solution. **But if you are firm, if you are clear, if you follow through regularly, it *will* work, I promise.** And soon, when you take them to the parking lot of school or wherever else you need to go in the world, you will be able to trust them to make the right decisions without you holding their hand.

CHAPTER EIGHT

The Lionhearted Child

Self-esteem

"Here's a bumper sticker I'd like to see: 'We are the proud parents of a child whose self-esteem is sufficient that he doesn't need us promoting his minor scholastic achievements on the back of our car.'"

—George Carlin

CHECKLIST

☑ Do you discourage clingy behavior?

☑ Do you avoid labels?

☑ Does your child have friends? Is she invited to friends' houses for playdates and birthday parties?

☑ Can your child cope with criticism?

☑ Is your child allowed to be himself? Is that good enough for you?

- ☑ Is your child liked by her teacher? Is that a good relationship?
- ☑ Do you help your child navigate his strengths and weaknesses?
- ☑ Does your child have a nervous habit like nail-biting or teeth-grinding, or complain about stomachaches?
- ☑ Is your child sad or withdrawn?
- ☑ Is your child being bullied?
- ☑ Does your child have chores and responsibilities that match her capabilities?
- ☑ Is your child allowed to complete tasks, imperfectly, on her own?
- ☑ Do you praise more than you admonish? Do you recognize when your child does something well?
- ☑ Do you avoid talking about your child's behavior in front of her?
- ☑ Do you avoid favoritism?
- ☑ Do you role model a positive/healthy self-esteem?
- ☑ Do you show love and affection daily?
- ☑ Do you react appropriately to your child's disappointment or failures?

There's a scene in the comedy movie *The Change-Up* in which a school-aged girl is complaining to her parents that her poem did not earn top recognition. The dad (who's actually the dad's best friend stuck in the dad's body) remarks, "Your poem, which I've never seen, is much better than this other kid's, whose poem I have also never seen." The point, of course, is that absurdities of modern parenting can best be seen through the eyes of a body imposter. Or, I would argue, a nanny.

Self-esteem sets off a hotbed of emotions in the United States, and I believe all of the focus on it doesn't serve children or their parents. Parents today parent as if they are imagining their child in therapy twenty years out, and they want to come off well to some imagined future therapist. In fact, though she was joking (I hope!), Michelle Pfeiffer articulated this very thought when she said, "My husband and I just do the best we can, and hold our breath, and hope we've set aside enough money to pay for our kids' therapy." As a result of this self-consciousness, parents are often *too* quick to praise, *too* quick to let a child off the hook if the child is feeling bad, *too* quick to give a medal whether the child's won or lost. Feeling bad sometimes is part of growing up. Losing sometimes is part of growing up. Building self-esteem should be about helping a child feel okay when he's lost, not creating an illusion that he's won.

I visited a middle school recently and watched the teachers set up for a basketball game for the kids. I noticed they didn't use a scoreboard and asked them why. "It upsets some of the kids when the games get competitive," explained one. I couldn't understand it. Isn't a game by its very nature competitive? I brought it up with my friend Barb, a swim coach, who shared her own "scoreboard moment" with me. As many coaches do, she divides children into "A" and "B" relay teams for competitions so that they can swim with others at a comparable skill level, but one mum took issue with this. She approached Barb after a lesson and asked her to rename the divisions the "A team" and "A-minus team." Being part of something labeled "B team," she worried, was hurting her daughter's feelings.

Barb was taken aback, to say the least. Fifteen years ago, when

Barb started coaching (and I started nannying), parents who suggested that their child's delicate constitution required such adjustments and euphemisms were seen as oddballs, and their requests were met with a raised eyebrow and a firm "no." Now, not even a generation later, Barb and I are astounded to find that parents like these are everywhere.

Somehow, over the last fifteen years, parents have increasingly embraced the idea that rules are for other people's children, and that bending them to make things easier in the short-term is a good idea. But being a good parent doesn't mean keeping your children happy in every moment. It means raising them to be healthy, independent, gracious, and happy as adults. It means setting them up for success, not a rude awakening. When short-term and long-term happiness appear to conflict, the choice is easy.

Overprotectors like this swim-team mum fall at one end of the spectrum. There's another end, though, where parents don't praise their children enough. I would argue British parents are particularly guilty of withholding praise. There's a cultural humble pie we've all eaten in England, wherein it's all about Hugh Grant–esque self-deprecation. Some might say it's part of our charm, but I think it's a problem in England. We have much to learn from Americans on this point. It's all about balance—kids *should* get a pat on their back if they excel in a math exam!

Through this chapter's checklist, my greatest hope is that you will see what I've seen from living and working with children on both sides of the pond. That is, I hope you will see the magical balance, that you will give your child the encouragement and praise he needs to be himself, and the tools to handle the disappointments and hard knocks that will inevitably come his way.

☑ *Do you discourage clingy behavior?*

Separation anxiety—most often characterized by kids clinging to their mums in public and freaking out if Mum or Dad walks out of the room or even out of sight—is entirely normal. For some children it's just a phase, and it can rear its head at any time, or even several times throughout childhood. When it *is* a problem, however, it's easy to tell and should be addressed. If your five-year-old cannot be dropped off without crying at a daycare that she attends each day, that's a problem. If your toddler routinely asks to be held by you as you're walking about the house, and freaks out every time you need to go to the bathroom, that's a problem. These children aren't comfortable operating in the world without you immediately by their side, and that's an issue. To remedy it, follow these three guidelines:

1. As I've written in previous chapters, make sure that you are building up your child to spend more and more time independently. Engage him by playing blocks together, and then explain that you are going to step away for a moment to change the laundry or write an e-mail. Extend the moments slowly until he is comfortable playing by himself for as long as a half hour at a time, or longer if he's older.

2. If your child is overly frightened of things such as a cleaning lady entering your hotel room while you are all there, or the loud noise of a fire truck passing by, then assure him that everything's okay, but do not go overboard in comforting him. That only reinforces that he was correct to be afraid, when in fact there was nothing to be afraid of. Say, "Oh, did that scare you? Don't fret, that was just the hotel cleaning lady, it's fine." If he continues to seek

comfort, try to gently detach and yet be encouraging—acknowledge his fear but let him know he's okay.

3. Give him opportunities to be without you. He needs to learn to adapt to your absence; otherwise you'll be smothered. I once worked with a family where the mum did not feel she could ever leave her three kids. If she left them at home with their dad to run an errand by herself, they would scream the whole time she was gone. There was nothing *wrong* with Dad, the kids just weren't used to being with him, and the parents hadn't made that okay for them. It was a terrible situation, wherein the mum never got any time with her friends or for herself outside of the home, the Dad felt inadequate and helpless, and the kids felt insecure. The mum needed to fight her urge to give in and always just stay home. She and the dad needed to communicate with the kids about what was going to happen and what behavior they expected, and they also needed to take away the anxiety of mum leaving: "You're going to stay with Daddy and you are going to have so

PARENT TIP

Before we had kids, we had a puppy, and my husband and I took him to obedience class. The instructor explained that before leaving the puppy for work, we shouldn't fuss over him, but should say very cheerfully, "Good-bye, George!" which would make him feel at ease with our parting. (His name, by the way, wasn't George, but that was the example the instructors used.) Now that we have kids and our littlest always fusses when we leave, we've gotten into the habit of saying, "Good-bye, George!" It reinforces the lesson for us, the cheerful tone is helpful for our daughter, and it's also a particular signal that we're going but will be back later. She was a little confused about who George was at first, but ultimately just thought we were funny.

much fun! Then Mummy's coming home and we're all going to play a game." The absolute worst things to do are to give in and stay with them or to inordinately coddle them before you leave, which sends the signal that all is not going to be well. Instead be empowering, encouraging, and reassuring.

☑ *Do you avoid labels?*

Nothing makes me more furious than parents who label their child. This subject takes me again to swim class, where I recently took one of my charges. Five-year-old twin boys also attended the class. Every time an adult talked about the twin named Will—whether it was the swim teacher, his nanny, or his parent—she was clearly labeling him. "How was Will today?" "Oh, just a nightmare all day." "Well, that's Will for you." I would watch Will walk around with a long face. He was so grumpy and miserable, and he was five years old! It hurt me to watch. I have no doubt that Will did not behave well—I saw it firsthand—but that wasn't because Will was a problem; it was because his caregivers were. Most likely, he cried more as a baby, or early on responded to discipline or boundaries in a less compliant way than his twin, and from that point he was labeled "the difficult one." These caregivers let Will down and created a self-fulfilling prophecy for him, as kids more often than not *will* conform to their labels.

Perhaps I learned my greatest lessons about the dangers of labeling from a mum I used to work for, Emily. Two of her sons were diagnosed as having behavioral problems when they were in high school, and one was even medicated for several weeks. In the end, though, Emily wasn't comfortable with the labels assigned to her children. Never one to think her children walked on water, her gut nevertheless told her that her boys were normal. They clearly weren't perfect, but that didn't mean they had ADHD or Tourette's or whatever the school psychologists felt they had. She felt they needed to start with more rest, more exercise, and a better diet, and to get to the root of the problem instead of putting a Band-Aid over it. The school psychologists disagreed and let her know this.

Emily's predicament is not uncommon. The diagnosis of ADHD in children has risen by 41 percent in the past decade, and many who care for children—myself included—think that it's *over*-diagnosed.* Children are labeled for exhibiting normal kid behavior, and it's a travesty. A friend of mine refers to the phenomenon as "medicated, not educated." Dr. Jerome Groopman, a professor of medicine at Harvard and the author of *How Doctors Think*, would back me up. He told the *New York Times*, "There's a tremendous push where if the kid's behavior is thought to be quote-unquote abnormal—if they're not sitting quietly at their desk—that's pathological, instead of just childhood."†

Emily's response was a credit to her; it is so difficult to be stuck in the middle of medical experts and your own gut instinct as a parent. Her boys were indeed normal, she never permitted them to be labeled by the school, and they very quickly grew out of whatever behavioral hiccups they'd been experiencing. But for her eldest, those three weeks he'd been on medication came back to haunt him. He desperately wanted to be a pilot as he grew older, and participated in loads of flight training. But when the flight school pulled his medical files and saw he'd been prescribed Aderall, a stimulant, those dreams of becoming a pilot were dashed. Labels can stick with children for the rest of their lives. They can affect and limit their choices.

I have never been in another place where medication is so easily given as it is in the U.S. It makes me furious, in part because I see

---

* Alan Schwarz and Sarah Cohen, "A.D.H.D. Seen in 11% of U.S. Children as Diagnoses Rise," *New York Times*, March 31, 2013.

† Ibid.

EMMA TIP

You can't control everything, and strangers and family members alike will make comments *to* your child and *about* your child that perhaps you wish they wouldn't. Don't worry that just because Grandpa calls your toddler a "bruiser" in front of him, that the toddler is going to become one. Understand that some talk like this is normal—people love to compare siblings' dispositions, for instance, more to remark on how strange it is that two beings with the same parents could be so different than anything else. Much of it is harmless, and once you have an ear primed to listen for it, you'll easily be able to tell if it's frequent, and if there's a danger of it being self-fulfilling.

it as a similar pathology as that which plunks kids in front of the television too easily, or gives them the candy they're demanding: **Medication is a quick fix, not a real solution. We must pull up our socks and figure out what the root of the problem is.** If your child is anxious, by all means put him on medication if nothing else has worked. But also take a close, hard look at why he might be anxious. If you're too busy to do so, then that's an excellent sign you need to slow down!

☑ Does your child have friends? Is she invited to friends' houses for playdates and birthday parties?

Friendships and other close relationships are crucial to building a child's self-esteem, and while it's normal for your child to be left out on occasion, if she is the one who is *always* left out, it's cause for further investigation as to why. It's not good enough to say, "Oh, she's just shy—she'll grow out of it." You need to ensure that she's learning how to build good friendships, not only to teach her skills she'll need later in life but also for her present well-being. If a child is horrible and doesn't know how to behave, if she's rude or disruptive, she *will* be excluded from playdates and birthday parties. No one wants their child hanging out with a child who doesn't know how to behave. This is an important example of how parents do their children a great disservice by trying too hard to make them happy. You may think you're doing the best thing for your child by giving her everything she wants in life, but you're setting her up for failure socially. You don't want her to end up without friends because she's insufferable.

Note, too, that it's okay if she doesn't have a dozen best friends; many children (and adults) are more comfortable with one or two close friends than an entourage. And really, one or two close friends are all it takes.

EMMA TIP

As much as I think it hurts self-esteem if a child is *never* included in birthday parties, that does not mean I think they *always* should be. I strongly disagree with some schools' policies that if a child is having a birthday party, he must invite his whole class. That's unfair to the child, and unfair to the parents sponsoring the party. Instead, use birthday parties and their requisite invitations as a means to teach good social skills. Teach the party-thrower to be discreet so as not to hurt the feelings of those not invited. If your child is left out of a party and feels badly about it, teach him that sometimes that's the way these things go—there are parties he *will* be invited to, too, and not being invited to this party is not a statement about him as a person. Let him know it's okay to feel bad but important not to make too much of it. This is the long-view approach, for even if you can protect him as a kindergartner, you won't be able to make the girl he wants to take to prom accept his invitation twelve years down the road. Start building the skills for resiliency when he's young, and he'll learn how to adapt.

☑ Can your child cope with criticism?

Children naturally want to please their parents, which is a lovely state of affairs. It is reassuring when a child feels badly about lying, for instance, or for breaking a special plate because he was careless. But if a child falls to pieces every time he's corrected, it's time to work on thickening his skin. You can't mollycoddle him each time he feels poorly for getting in trouble—that only reinforces his reaction.

Instead, model the behavior you want to see. Point it out when *you* make mistakes, and make a show of letting your child know that it's okay to mess up and does not mean you are a bad person. Show him how to learn from his errors and move on, and you will be setting him up well for the future.

I often find American adults to be oversensitive, and I believe it stems from the fact that parents sugarcoat everything for their kids from a very young age. While the shouting and horridness of some high-pressure work environments (medicine and law come to mind!) are awful, we mustn't go so far in the other direction that each performance review, each conversation where constructive criticism is applied, is cause for bringing out the Kleenex.

☑ Is your child allowed to be himself? Is that good enough for you?

Albert Einstein said, "Everybody is a genius. But if you judge a fish by its ability to climb a tree, it will live its whole life believing that it is stupid." Projecting your own desires or a general standard on your child is one of the most detrimental things you can do.

I have a good friend, Mary, who has the most well-behaved son, Andrew. British and trained as a nanny herself, Mary has managed to set the bar high for her son's behavior, and he's met it well. As he's grown older, however, she does struggle with *others'* expectations of him. Andrew's dad is an NBA star, so everyone in their circle of friends always assumed that Andrew would be an amazing player as well. The truth is, though Andrew loved going to basketball games and watching his dad play, he *wasn't* a good player. He was particularly sensitive to the perceptions of those who watched him on the court. He could hear them express disappointment that maybe he didn't have the "touch" after all. He moved further and further away from wanting to play. He wanted to play soccer, and so that's what he played. His parents never pushed basketball. This year, however, he suddenly announced that he wanted to try basketball again, but he thought he needed a coach. They got him one, and he's loving basketball and has become really good at it. He might not ever be as strong a player as his dad, but his choice to pursue it or not is up to him, and it's a choice he feels comfortable with. The lesson here is that Andrew gets to be Andrew, and ought not be compared to anyone.

☑ Is your child liked by her teacher? Is that a good relationship?

If your child talks about her teacher negatively, or claims not to care that the teacher doesn't like her, don't let it go as a by-product of youth. It matters too much. Your child does not have to be Head Girl, but if she is feeling discounted or disliked by her teacher—someone who has a great deal of authority and influence over her—then that's a red flag worth paying attention to. She might be internalizing the disappointment of that relationship, and it might be affecting the way she feels about herself in the world, or about school in general. Get involved. Don't go to the teacher and say, "You need to make my daughter feel better about herself!" but you might need to help put the relationship on a stronger course. You can stand by the teacher's decision to discipline your child, for instance, while also making sure that your child has *positive* encounters with that teacher.

Make sure that the teacher is not labeling your child. In a famous 1960s study, psychologists Robert Rosenthal and Lenore Jacobson showed that when teachers learned certain students had more potential to excel, those students were treated accordingly, and did in fact test better.* So how can you tell if your child's teacher is labeling him, and what can you do about it?

Often labeling is obvious: the teacher will tell you straight-out that your child is a big problem or will offer some other blanket designation. But sometimes you have to look deeper. Most children excel in *something*—be it athletics, math, or just being a good class citizen. If the feedback you're getting from his teacher is consistently and wholly negative, then you must ask why that is. Get involved, ask questions, meet with the teacher as many times as you can in order to get things straightened out. If you are getting such a negative vibe about your child from that teacher, your child is getting it threefold. Try to remove your child from that class and have him start fresh with a new teacher, or if all else fails, make efforts to connect your child with another authority figure—perhaps a coach or a tutor—whose influence and feedback will be more positive.

I have a good friend who runs a boarding school for boys called Chelfham Mill. The boys in his school were all labeled with behavioral difficulties before they came to Chelfham, and what my friend learned is that for most of their lives, no one believed in these kids. Their parents thought they were bad kids, their teachers agreed, and they really never had a chance. Yet after a time at Chelfham—where the teachers are very strict but also loving, supportive, and encouraging—they thrive. Many of them are able to return to their schools back home, where they have a new outlook on themselves and on life in general. It just goes to show just how powerful expectations are, and how it's never too late to replace the negative ones.

---

* Robert Rosenthal and Lenore Jacobson, "Teachers' Expectancies: Determinants of Pupils' IQ Gains," *Psychological Reports*, August 1966.

☑ Do you help your child navigate his strengths and weaknesses?

Sometimes I'll think what a child has done is brilliant, but he'll shrug, look down, and say, "Oh, it's okay." Where is he getting that? He's not coming up with it on his own. If your child feels that nothing he does is good, or good enough, then he needs help recognizing his strengths and forgiving his weaknesses. First, make sure this message is not coming from you, even if indirectly. If he sees you being exceptionally hard on yourself, he will model that behavior in himself. If he sees himself constantly coming up short in your eyes, he will think he cannot do right. The bar, in this case, has been set too high for his well-being.

On the flip side, if your child wants to play baseball, but in practice sessions with him you can see that he's not terribly good, it's wrong to tell him he's a brilliant player. It sets him up for humiliation in front of others when he takes that first at-bat. Know that somebody in the world is going to be honest with your child, and it's better if it's you. This does not mean that you say, "Billy, you're quite a miserable baseball player," but perhaps you say, "Hitting the ball isn't really your strong point, so how can we help you get better? If you really want to do this, let's make a plan for practicing. If you

EMMA TIP

For children struggling with self-esteem, I like to play a cooperative game where I time them skating (or running or jumping) from one mark to another. The object of the game is for the children to beat their own score. When they don't beat their own scores, they often look to me to see if it's okay. The key is to keep it positive and make no big deal of the fact that the child didn't beat his highest score. It's amazing how much this helps a highly stressed child to relax. It's all about letting children make mistakes and focusing on efforts.

don't want to play baseball after all, we can figure out another area where you will really excel."

☑ Does your child have a nervous habit like nail-biting or teeth-grinding, or complain about stomachaches?

If nail-biting, teeth-grinding, or stomachaches are a frequent problem for your child, she may be stressed. Every child will have a stomachache on occasion and decide she doesn't want to go to school, so no need to fret should that happen. But if it's happening more often than not, it could be cause for concern. Be particularly mindful about her diet, routine, and sleep, and spend extra time with her to determine whether the problem is one that needs to be addressed.

☑ Is your child sad or withdrawn?

I don't see kids who are sad very often, and there's a good reason for that: children are not inherently withdrawn, nor should they be. Not every child is the life of the party, but if yours is residing most of the time within a shell, it's cause for immediate concern and attention.

☑ Is your child being bullied?

I once consulted with a family whose eight-year-old son was constantly wrestling with his little sisters. Though he did it in fun and not maliciously, he did not take "no" for an answer and he was too physical with them. I asked his parents if he was being bullied in school, and sure enough, he was. "What message have you given him about bullies?" I asked. "We've told him to fight," his parents said. In fact, the dad would even go out and tussle with him to make sure he was prepared. The parents did not see the connection between this bully message and the problem their son was having with his sisters at home.

As wonderful as children are, they also have the capacity to be horrible to one another. Even if your child has not yet encountered a bully, chances are good that he will. Teach your children to stand up for themselves, absolutely, but also teach them the proper channels in which to do so, and that physically fighting back is not a proper channel. From the time children are very small, they can be taught to say, "I don't like it when you hit me," or "Please give me back my toy. You didn't ask if you could take it and I'm still playing with it." If they're older, like this little boy, teach them to handle bullies by standing tall and verbalizing that they won't be treated unfairly. If the situation progresses, help them find the tools to deal with it, possibly by getting a teacher involved.

Far from these parents who encouraged their son to use his fists lies another extreme. These are the parents who overreact to any sign of bullying. One little boy I knew was called "stupid" out on the playground one day. His mum, incensed, marched into school and raised holy hell. It became a big spectacle, and only fed this little boy's strategy to get attention. It did not teach him how to stand up for himself, it did not teach him to be resilient and let things roll off ("sticks and stones may break my bones but names will never harm me"), it did not teach him how to handle these other kids so that he could play with them. All it taught him was that there was cause for concern, and that he needs his mum to come to his rescue each time he feels bad.

Bullying is an incredibly loaded topic these days, and I applaud the work of people like Dan Savage (cocreator of the "It Gets Better" anti-bullying campaign) and Lee Hirsch (director of the 2011 documentary, *Bully*) who are raising awareness about its effects. I also applaud programs in schools that teach children empathy and emphasize anti-bullying messages. There are too many children who are deeply damaged by chronic bullying. If a child feels sick each time he has to go to school, or spends his time there hiding, that is a travesty.

At the same time, we must be careful not to overreact and swing too far the other way, as did the mum whose son was called stupid once. There has always been an ounce of bullying at schools, children have always had to deal with it, and there are important lessons like resilience learned through doing so. We want to wrap our children in cotton wool to protect them, but a huge point here is to learn when it's appropriate and necessary to intervene, and when it is better to coach from a distance.

☑ **Does your child have chores and responsibilities that match her capabilities?**

Giving your child chores and responsibilities is an important step to helping her learn self-reliance, a critical piece of healthy self-esteem. Folding the laundry at five years old is a stepping-stone to cooking dinner at eight years old, and who knows? By the time she's ten, she might be putting computers together or designing an addition for the bathroom! But let's not get ahead of ourselves!

EMMA TIP

Getting your child to help other kids can really boost his self-esteem. If your child struggles athletically but excels academically, encourage him to sign up to tutor other children. Or if your child is sensitive and kind, encourage him to be a peer counselor for others. Give him a chance to shine by sharing what he does well with others, and encourage him to be a giving and loving human being. That in and of itself will build his spirit and sense of worth.

The key is to start slowly. Show your child how to do a task first, and do it with her. If something you ask is too difficult, the child will feel overwhelmed and not even try, or will give up halfway through, feeling defeated. If your child can never complete something you ask her to do, chances are good you are asking too much. While I can't emphasize enough the importance of knowing *your* child, there are some general guidelines. If we ask a one-year-old to put away all of his blocks, for instance, he's not going to be able to do it. But he can absolutely put one block away. A two-year-old can put five blocks away. Three-year-olds can put all of their blocks away. Here is a chart of common expectations you can use as a general guideline:

Fourteen to Eighteen Months	Two-Year-Olds	Three- to Four-Year-Olds	Five- to Eight-Year-Olds
• Put a book away • Put 2 or 3 blocks away • Put an item of clothing in the hamper • Hold a fork • Clear their plate • Say or sign "thank you"	• Put 3 or 4 books away • Put half their blocks away • Put all their clothes in a hamper • Clear their plate from the table and scrape off leftover food • Help wipe up their spills	• Put all their blocks away • Help tidy their toys and books • Help feed pets • Get dressed • Say "Thank you for a yummy dinner" • Take clothes off and put them in a laundry basket • Use a fork and spoon and start to use a knife	• Keep track of their shoes and schoolbag • Clean their room • Help fill and empty the dishwasher • Take off their clothes and put them in the hamper • Get themselves ready for bed • Say "thank you for a yummy dinner" while maintaining eye contact

☑ ***Is your child allowed to complete tasks, imperfectly, on her own?***

Imagine you've asked your four-year-old to make her bed. She complies (score one for mum!), tugs up her sheet and blanket, and puts her pillow and stuffed bear on top. The bed, alas, is lumpy and still looks pretty messy to you. Do you

a. fix it behind her, so she can see how to do it right;

b. fix it later, once she's at school and can't see you do it; or

c. praise her for making her bed as you asked, and leave the lumps alone?

The correct answer here is c. That doesn't preclude your working with her to improve her bed-making skills in the future, but not today, when she's just made it as best she can and feels proud of it. Perhaps the next day you say, "Shall we make your bed *together* today? My mum taught me some neat tricks to doing it, and I think you're old enough for me to show you." If she demurs, again, leave it be. She is relishing her independence and competence right now, and for the moment that's far more important than making her bed with hospital corners.

Similarly, if you're potty training your child, and he's put his underwear on by himself but they're on backward, let it go. The

EMMA TIP

Resist the urge not only to correct things done improperly but also to do things for your child that he can do himself. I've taken care of an eighteen-month-old who doesn't like wearing his socks when he takes a nap. Instead of just taking them off for him, which certainly would have been easier, I would ask him to do it. I would help him pull, but at least he was trying. Step in or out depending on how much your child is able to do himself, but always think of your job as one of guiding, not doing. Not only will you end up doing less and making your life easier in time, but you will build positive feelings of self-reliance.

next day you might teach him where the label is and what it means, but don't do it when he's so proud of his effort. Another common scenario is when children put their shoes on by themselves. More often than not, especially at first, they will put them on the wrong foot. Instead of saying, "Oops, your shoes are on the wrong feet again!" say, "Do you see anything funny about your feet right now?" **Letting him take the lead in taking care of himself does wonders for building his independence and self-esteem.**

☑ *Do you praise more than you admonish? Do you recognize when your child does something well?*

It is so easy to get caught up in correcting your child's manners or behaviors, that you can forget the importance of praise and acknowledgment. Remember that your child wants to please you, and will strive to repeat the behavior you love to see. Let her know when she's colored a lovely picture or been sweet with her sister or brother. Be as specific in acknowledging what she's done well as you are in explaining why she can't do something. "Great job" is empty praise, and isn't nearly as impactful as "That was so lovely when Anne came over and you asked her how her day was. Thank you for using excellent manners." If you don't acknowledge this behavior, your child won't bother to exhibit it. She will think she is only noticed when she behaves badly.

> PARENT TIP
>
> My husband and I try to ask our son for help a lot. "Liam, can you please bring Daddy his shoes?" He feels like he's helping us, he's very proud about it, and he also gets to have the reverse role of hearing us say "please" to him when we ask for something.

Note, too, that there is a difference between praise and acknowledgment. In the example above, the child is not being overly praised so much as her behavior is acknowledged. ("Thank you for using excellent manners.") It's the difference between saying, "You get a gold star!!" and saying "Hey, I see you when you behave well and I appreciate it."

☑ Do you avoid talking about your child's behavior in front of her?

Let's say you made a mistake at work. Your boss called you in and discussed it with you, and you paid the consequence. How would you feel if you then stood next to your boss in the lunchroom while he recounted your mistake to your colleagues? It would feel completely unfair: You already paid the price of your mistake, why should you do so again? Can't that arse just leave it be? Don't be the arse. If your child has gotten into trouble for something and he's already experienced the consequence and apologized, then do not talk about his mistake in front of him. An exception might be if you need to communicate with another caregiver about the consequence: "Laura had a tough day listening to Mummy today, so she's lost her dessert privileges." But if you are exasperated by Laura and you and your partner need to discuss a plan of attack, do not discuss it in front of her. Put yourself in her shoes and imagine how that would feel. Also, do not underestimate how much she can understand. You might think she's not paying attention when you are complaining to your husband about her behavior, or that the language you're using is over her head, but children are really quite brilliant. Assume that one way or the other, they get it, and be more discreet about where and when you have such conversations.

☑ Do you avoid favoritism?

Favoritism is another hot-button—perhaps even taboo—topic, and it might surprise you to know I see it happen *all the time.* Parents never say to me that they prefer one child to another. Parents often don't realize that they are favoring one child over the other. But they are, and the result is terrible.

Naturally, there are going to be different qualities you love about each of your children, and that is fine. But at the end of the day, you must nurture your children equally. If you are really interested in sports, for instance, and your son plays every sport under the sun while your daughter is more musical, it is only natural to gravitate toward your son's sporting events—to attend more of them, to ask him more questions about them, to practice tossing a ball with him. Do all of these things, but do them equally with your daughter. Attend as many of her recitals as his games. Ask her questions about her hobby and show a genuine curiosity to understand it. Take her to a musical performance as a special outing for the two of you. You may never embrace music as much as sports, but know that it affects her when your attention is split unequally. Be brutally honest with yourself about whether or not this is happening. It's not fair to expect her to understand that you love sports more than music, and she may come to believe that you love your son more than her.

Once I was called in to advise parents who were having difficulty with their daughter. She was bossy, she was obnoxious, and she was alienated by all of her friends. This girl also had a blue-eyed brother who could do no wrong, or at least that's what it seemed like. It became clear after spending time with this family that favoritism was a problem. The dad in particular was not giving his daughter the love and attention he was giving his son, and the daughter was crying out for his attention at every turn. Explaining to a parent that they are favoring a child is incredibly difficult—they do not want to hear it, and in fact, this father became hostile. It was such a pity, because he was really enforcing this terrible cycle. His daughter felt slighted by him, so acted out to get attention. Her parents expected her to be difficult, and she met those expectations.

☑ *Do you role model positive/healthy self-esteem?*

I can tell when mums or dads don't feel good about themselves. I see it in the way they dress, in the way they keep their homes. If they are prone to seeing the glass as half empty and themselves as helpless victims, they are passing on that worldview to their children. Instead of teaching their children that they can handle whatever life throws their way, the parents are teaching them helplessness and hopelessness. If you suspect you fall into this category, the best course would be to get help from a friend or therapist. If you are unwilling or if it's not possible, then be very aware and careful about the messages you're sending to your children. Show them that sometimes life is good, sometimes it's bad, but ultimately you are strong in who you are.

☑ *Do you show love and affection daily?*

Brits are not huggers. We're simply not. I didn't learn how to give a good, meaningful hug until I came to America (although funnily enough, it was my Peruvian friend who taught me!). Now I love a good hug. It is such a gesture of warmth, goodwill, and humanity, and I wish those in my native land would learn to let down their guard a bit more and open themselves up for a big squeeze. This cultural trait passes over to our parenting. British parenting is not as warm and affectionate as American parenting, and I think that's a shame.

Even in America, though, I see families all the time where the kids are not touched. Hugging, cuddling, tickling, and kissing equal nurturing, and children need it. Saying "How are you feeling?" is a lovely way of showing you care for someone's well-being. If you weren't parented this way yourself, it can be difficult to get used to. You might be uncomfortable showing affection. But push yourself out of your comfort zone, because your children need it!

Now there are some who will argue that withholding such proclamations of love and signs of affection is beneficial to children. The Tiger Mothers out there feel it pushes them harder to achieve, and in and of itself sets a higher bar. There are even some who were raised this way who claim that their fervent desire to secure their parents' hard-won approval drove them to the success they achieved. Perhaps this is true for some, but are they really, truly emotionally healthy? Are they successful in life or only in business or wealth? As I've said, children have an innate desire to make their parents proud—we don't need to tear them down to instill this in them.

☑ Do you react appropriately to your child's disappointment or failures?

Assume your child has worked incredibly hard for an upcoming exam. She's put in every free hour to study and you know she's done her best, but she gets a B. Do you say,

a. "Oh that's an amazing grade, congrats!"

b. "I'm really proud of you, I know you worked your hardest. It's not the A you were looking for but it's still a good grade."

c. "I'm really disappointed—you're incredibly smart and should've gotten an A."

The right answer here is b and parents get it wrong more often than you'd think! For instance, I counseled a family whose ten-year-old daughter, Maggie, was really struggling. She was anxious and nervous, and I was asked to put on my detective hat and investigate why. On one of the days I was visiting, Maggie came home and informed her mother she didn't get the role she had wanted in the school play. Maggie was disappointed, and so was the mum. In fact, the mum was really disappointed, and labored over the *"whys"* and the *"this stinks!"* much more than she should have. I couldn't tell if the mum was disappointed *for* Maggie or if she was disappointed *in* Maggie.

Denying disappointment altogether is no good, and it would not have sufficed for the mum to say, "Oh well! It's just a play, let's move on and do something else." That wouldn't have allowed Maggie to process through what she was feeling, and might have increased her bad feelings about herself, because her mum was delegitimizing her disappointment.

The middle ground, of course, is the correct one.

The mum should have listened to and empathized with Maggie's feelings, and then helped her to feel good about her efforts. Maggie was courageous for putting herself on the line and auditioning for the play—good for her! It is understandably disappointing that she didn't get the part she wanted, but it seems like the part she did get will be fun, and perhaps she'll get more of a role in another play in the future. In other words, the mum had to make the rejection okay for Maggie, without denying its existence altogether.

You know when your children are doing their best. If their best effort results in a B, that is what it is. But if their best efforts could result in an A, yet their application of effort is lacking and earns them a B, then a parent has every right to be disappointed and to let their children know it.

PARENT TIP

We talk about how we (the parents) aren't perfect, and how we are good at some things but not so good at others, and how we are always working on getting better. We try to verbalize when we make mistakes and make light of them if they are minor ones. Our older son now says, "Ooops! That was just a mistake" when he goofs up but is able to realize that it is really just part of life.

Holding the Line

Volumes have been written about how to nurture your child's self-esteem, and I'm confident that between Oprah and Dr. Phil, weeks on end of television programming have been devoted to the subject as well. And yet as well versed as parents and child care providers are in all of the latest self-esteem terminology, they nevertheless are making simple mistakes, daily—mistakes like picking up a child each time he falls, mistakes like obviously favoring one child over another, mistakes like labeling a child. Before you invest in your child's future therapist, Michelle Pfeiffer–style, think about the simple habits you have. If they're not in keeping with what you've read in this chapter, break them.

CHAPTER NINE

Quieting the Rabble

Quality Time

"Other things may change us, but we start and end with the family."

—Anthony Brandt

CHECKLIST

☑ Do you know your child well?

☑ Is your child getting enough attention from each parent?

☑ Is your child having fun when he's with you? Are you making small moments count versus having it all be task-driven?

☑ Are you spending time with your child each day?

☑ Are you saying hello and good-bye?

☑ Are you truly present with your child, without a smartphone, newspaper, or other distraction?

- ☑ Are mealtimes family time?
- ☑ Do you focus on your child straightaway after an absence?
- ☑ Do you know how to be with your child?
- ☑ Do you *express* interest in your child's hobbies?
- ☑ Does your family have traditions?
- ☑ Are you letting go of expectations and letting your child's special activities be *hers*?

A MUM I WORK with fully supported the idea of quality time and blocked off several hours each day to spend with her son. And yet he still acted out and made all kinds of appeals for her attention through bad behavior. Mum was beside herself trying to figure out *why*. This completely well-meaning mum needed a small tweak. The time she spent with her son was all shuttling to soccer class and kung fu and playdates. They were in the car together for long periods, but often they were listening to the radio, and they weren't looking at each other. All she needed to do was spend twenty minutes regularly sitting across from him, coloring, talking, or sharing a treat at a coffee shop. In reality, she would have been much better off having him be part of a carpool, saving her time with him for when they could both be fully present and engaged with each other.

A self-employed mum I know was determined not to work full-time, and so she took off one day a week to spend with her two small kids. The problem was that on that single day she also tried to do all of the family's housekeeping, to take each child aside for some one-on-one time, to keep up with her e-mail, and to stay on top of work so that she could get everything done she needed to in just four workdays. Again, this mum needed a tweak. Like the shuttle-mum, she was focusing too much on quantity of time and not enough on quality. She ended up shifting her schedule so that she works five days, does a little housekeeping or an errand in the mornings once the kids have left but before she starts work, and picks the kids up from daycare earlier. She now spends more time focused on them, and in a way that she can bring her most playful, least distracted self. Of course, not all parents are fortunate enough to have such control over their work schedules, but the point remains: Don't assume that quantity equals quality.

Quality time might be the single most common issue that parents miss. Smartphones and television and newspapers create a very real barrier between us and our children, even when we are sitting in close proximity. I see this all the time during meals, where parents may sit with their children but be occupied with the newspaper, cell phone, or laptop. They tell me, "I spend quality time with Karen/Jimmy/Zoe—we always have breakfast together, no matter what." *But proximity is not quality.* This becomes especially important if you see your children for only a couple of hours a day, which is the case for many parents with older children. Make that time count. If you're not putting in the time, they may go elsewhere, and with perhaps a less-than-favorable influence.

Aside from helping you recognize what quality time *really* consists of, this chapter will fill you with ideas of things you can do with your children, whether they're babies or elementary-schoolers, whether you're high energy or low, whether you're a hipster or a bookworm. That's another frequently misunderstood idea about quality time—it doesn't have to be about doing kid stuff!

☑ *Do you know your child well?*

Let's begin with a quiz about how well you know your child.

1. What's your child's favorite . . .
    - Toy?
    - Food?
    - Book?
    - Lullaby/song?
    - Color?
    - Activity?

2. What comforts him when he's . . .
    - Sick?
    - Sad?
    - Upset?

3. What are your child's cues when she's uncomfortable in an environment or situation?

4. What triggers your child to have a meltdown?

5. What signals does your child display when . . .
    - Hungry?
    - Tired?
    - Bored?

6. If your child is preschool age or older, do you know who his friends are?

7. Who does your child sit next to at school?

8. Who and what does your child play with at recess?

Answer these questions honestly. How many have you left blank? You might examine why, and consider it a sign that you're not spending enough quality time with your child.

☑ Is your child getting enough attention from each parent?

If there are two parents at home, *both* must spend quality time with their children. It's not uncommon to find a family where they've agreed Mum will do most of the child care while Dad is primarily responsible for earning money, or vice versa. This is a perfectly fine arrangement, but only to a point. No one gets a complete pass.

A family I worked with in Studio City, California, had this very problem. Mum was spending loads of time with the children, but the dad was checked out, absent, even when he was physically present. The dad worked from home, but he had his laptop up constantly, and could zone out even the most hyper, outrageous behavior on the part of his kids. Children feel that absence, and in this case their behavior reflected it. They were frankly little monsters—they would scream and run around inside and tear things apart. The parents felt the kids were out of control, and they were. But the kids were also saying something very simple, albeit loudly and messily: "Pay attention to us."

I worked with the mum on being more authoritative and setting and keeping clear limits. She did an amazing job, and the kids really began to respond to her. But many of the problems with the household remained. For the kids to really settle down, Dad needed to participate as well. I pulled him aside and asked what was going on. He talked about how difficult it was to work at home, how it was hard to set boundaries with his work, and how often he viewed his children as obstructions to getting done what he needed to get done. I could see his point—they were obstructions, no doubt. He didn't want to spend time with them because they were screaming all the time, but they were screaming all the time because he wasn't spending time with them. It was a never-ending circle. If Dad was to continue working at home, he needed to set some clear rules with his work and with his children. Dad needed to spend time with them, fully focusing on them first, and then he could explain that he

EMMA TIP

If your child is

- blurting loud noises for no reason
- frequently talking over you, your spouse, or his siblings, or
- constantly underfoot,

then there's an excellent chance that he's actually craving attention. In one family I worked with, the potty-trained son would pee every time his mum came into the room—he wanted her to pay attention to him, and he knew his "accidents" would do the trick. If you are having any number of these problems on a consistent basis with your child, tweak your routine so that you are spending more one-on-one, quality time with him. **Chart the undesirable behaviors and the time you're spending together (or lack thereof) to see the correlation.**

needed an hour to work and he needed them to be quiet during that time. The kids were old enough that they could entertain themselves for quite a long time. Once they were full up with his attention, they let him work. It improved his relationship with them greatly, it improved their behavior, and it improved the marriage.

☑ Is your child having fun when he's with you? Are you making small moments count versus having it all be task-driven?

One thing I regret so much about families today is that there isn't enough joy. Children by nature laugh—a lot. If your child is not laughing with you, why is that? Most often it's because everyone is just rushing, rushing, rushing all the time. "Get your shoes on," "Get in the car," "Get to school," "Get to soccer practice," "Get to dinner," "Get into the bath," "Get your room picked up," and "Get to bed." As renowned columnist and author Anna Quindlen wrote, "The biggest mistake I made [as a parent] is the one that most of us make while doing this. I did not live in the moment enough. . . . I wish I had not been in such a hurry to get on to the next thing: dinner, bath, book, bed. I wish I had treasured the doing a little more and the getting it done a little less."*

If your child is young, there is an excellent chance you're already spending a lot of time with her, but it's probably time in which you're combing her hair, or giving her a bath, or helping her dress. Make these times quality times—as you help her get dressed, ask her what she's excited about in the day ahead. As you bathe her at night, play a game in the bath, or talk to her about her day. Don't rush these little moments or discount them— they are valuable, and can be meaningful, too.

Designated "fun time" is also why vacations are so brilliant, right? On vacation, you can let your kids wear their bathing suits all day, and the only choice is whether to go to the pool or for a dip in the lake. Our lives back home are busy, and there's not always that much we can do about it. We need to make a living, our kids need to go to school, grass needs to be mowed, groceries need to be bought, and so on. Unless we are to become surf bums (which comes with its own set of problems, believe me), we are where we are. We might not be able or even want to throw our busy lives by the side of the road and become fun-loving hippies, but there are *some* things we can do. We can rush less. We can schedule less. We can commit to spending one afternoon a week together having fun. Or we can simply do what Quindlen suggests, and just live in the moment. If you're giving your child a bath, treasure the doing. If you're reading a bedtime story, don't just rush through monotonously reading, but stop and savor where you are. Really look at the pictures with your child. Ask her questions about it. Listen to her answers, and relish the sound of her small voice telling you. When you are in that space with her, she will feel it, and she will treasure it. So will you.

---

* Anna Quindlen, *Loud and Clear* (New York: Ballantine, 2005).

☑ Are you spending time with your child each day?

Assuming that you don't share custody and don't travel loads for work, you ought to spend time with your child each and every day. How *much* time you're able to spend will vary based on your schedule and your family's needs as well as your child's—and I can't assign you a number of minutes. The important point here is that the time be put in *consistently*. Of course there will be days when you get home late or meet a friend after work, but try to make sure it's not two nights in a row or more than a couple of times a week. Twenty minutes, two times, each and every day goes miles, actually, toward enforcing your consistent role in your child's life.

☑ Are you saying hello and good-bye?

Gretchen Rubin, author of *The Happiness Project* and *Happier at Home*, had a goal to make greetings in her household matter. She felt it was important that when someone in their family left the apartment, or came back to it, that should be noted. Others should stop what they were doing to give that person a good-bye or hello kiss. I think this is brilliant! It's a way of saying, "Hey, you're important to me." It's a way of staying connected to one another. I often tell parents that even if they need to leave for work before their child is up, they should go into the child's room, kiss her good-bye, and wish her a good day. Over the years, this adds up to a lot of moments, and takes only seconds. The same is true for bedtime. Tuck your children into bed each and every night if you can. How you end your day is as important as how you start it. Let it be your voice and loving touch she hears saying goodnight at the end of the day.

☑ Are you truly present with your child, without a smartphone, newspaper, or other distraction?

Write down how much time you spend with your child on a normal workday. Say you've jotted down something like an hour in the morning, and two or three in the evening. Okay, let's look more closely. How is that time spent? How much of it are you on the phone? How much of it are you watching TV? How much of it are you reading something on your own? How much of it are you in the car? **I constantly tell parents that the best present is your presence, so make sure you are really and truly present.** The time you spend making phone calls, reading the newspaper, and even checking your smartphone has a place, but it doesn't count as quality time. You don't need to be completely zeroed in on your child from the second you're all home at the end of the day until it's time for bed. Rather, you need to understand the difference between time together and quality time together, and you need to make quality the priority.

☑ Are mealtimes family time?

As I covered in Chapter Four, so many wonderful benefits come from having a healthy meal routine. If you feel you have no time with your children, determine that you will have a family dinner one day a week and nothing can interfere with that, period. No phones, no computers, just sitting together, eating and talking. It can be just thirty minutes, and it can be take-out noodles. But make it happen.

Here's another way to look at it: even though everyone is busy, everyone must eat! So even if you can't make time for a coloring activity or a walk around the block, you can and have to make time for a meal together. Whether it's breakfast, lunch, or dinner, sit down with your kids and make it quality time.

☑ Do you focus on your child straightaway after an absence?

If you've been gone for the day, take care to have the time when you reunite with your child be quality time. I see little kids' faces just melt when Mum or Dad comes home and immediately starts to make phone calls or takes on an errand. Your child misses you when you're away—honor that, give him your undivided attention, and focus on your reunion before moving on to something else. He will be much more accommodating once you've filled up his tank!

☑ Do you know how to be with your child?

Realize that no parent is good at all the stages of their child's development. Some are better with babies or toddlers; some are better when their children are teenagers. Don't be too hard on yourself if you don't love a certain stage, but do try to get into the spirit of it and make it work for both you and your child. Many parents turn to their smartphones or avoid playtime altogether because they find activities like make-believe or playing dolls boring. I get it! But there's no reason you can't find joint activities around something *you* enjoy. I've found that what parents want the most when it comes to quality time is ideas. To that end, here are loads of my favorite ideas to suit any mood:

WHEN YOU'RE TIRED

- When one dad is feeling too tired to run around with his kids, he pulls out a stopwatch and times how fast or how long his kids can do something. It's low energy for dad and high energy for the kids. Win-win!
- Sit at the table and play with Play-Doh, color, or read stories.

- Do puzzles!
- Go someplace calm: I love taking kids to the library when I'm tired. It gets the kids out the house, but it doesn't take a lot of energy. They're normally excited to read new books they haven't seen before and I get to sit and read.
- Build something with Legos or building blocks. Kids love to build. And younger children love to knock things down.

WHEN THERE'S ENERGY TO BURN

- Dancing! I'm a huge fan of dance parties. I put on some fun music and I get up and dance with children. Everyone rocks out and practices their dance moves. It's a lot of fun and the kids can blow off steam.
- "If it's a nice day," one mum told me, "my son and I will bike to school and home together. It adds a bit of time on to the day—usually meaning I'm a little late to work and early out—but he loves it and it seems like he's more open with me about his day when we ride home together. If we have extra time, we'll take the long way through the park and along the lake and we can get a few extra minutes together without my husband or daughter."
- Pillow fights. Feel free to set the parameters around this as you see fit!
- Running. One dad I know loves to run with his four-year-old. They don't go fast enough for Dad to get a good workout, but it's still exercise, and as the four-year-old grows older, he'll probably beat his dad's best time.
- Playing games. For young children, take a wind-up musical toy and listen to it, saying "Music." Then hide the musical toy

under a pillow and say, "Where is the music?" Help your child find it. Give hoorays and claps when she finds it, then hide it again across the room so she has to crawl to get it.

WHEN YOU HAVE CHORES TO DO

- Have children help you make a list for the grocery store. Involve them in the shopping. Let them hold the list and help you find items on it. Let them choose one special fruit or ingredient they'd like to cook with.
- If you have laundry to fold, have them hand you matching socks or things to fold. They can also sort clothes by guessing what clothes belong to which family member. One mum I know loves to make laundry time dress-up time: everyone puts on a tiara or skirt, they put on music, and they dance around as they put away clothes.
- Garden together. Children love to water and dig. One mum used to give her son a bug jar and he would collect snails that had gathered in her pots, which he loved!
- If you're making the bed, have your child help pull up the sheets and fluff the pillows.
- In one family, the dad likes to hold up his daughter while Mum and Dad cook, and he explains what the parents are doing. I recommend using pods, which are somewhat like kitchen stools, only safer. They allow your child to reach the counter without you constantly having to worry that he'll fall backward. Depending on his age, he can tear lettuce, or mix ingredients into a bowl, or even measure ingredients or wash dishes.
- Another mum plays a game with her seven-year-old daughter based on the television show *Chopped!* On the show, the contestants are given three ingredients that they have to

make something delicious with, quickly. So she puts simple ingredients such as peanut butter, jelly, and graham crackers in a basket and covers it with a cloth. She has her daughter remove the cloth, then make something with the ingredients while the timer ticks down. It's teaching the seven-year-old to love and appreciate cooking.

- One mum who has two dogs loves bringing her kids along to walk them: "They each get a dog to walk and they tend to get along really well when we go on walks where they have some sort of responsibility. Usually we have some destination and then the kids can play together for a few minutes before walking home."
- One little girl loves to watch her dad fix things, and he usually lets her help. The mum says, "It's ridiculously cute to watch their matching plumber sandwiches poking out from under the sink."

WHEN YOU FEEL CREATIVE

There may be times when you are feeling artistic, whether it's of the musical variety or more craft oriented! Consider these activities:

- Playing music. Andrew adores music, and loves to sit with his seven-year-old son, Jack, and play records. Sometimes Andrew will play the guitar and Jack will sing or play drums. If they really get excited about the same band, Andrew will take Jack to a concert if the band/singer happens to come to town. At the time of this writing, Jack is really into the Beatles and he and Andrew are looking forward to seeing Paul McCartney when he comes to their city on tour.
- Giving your baby a wooden spoon and encouraging her to bang it on the floor. Do it together and sing your favorite songs.

- Making root beer. Matt loves to make and bottle root beer, and has taught his ten-year-old and eight-year-old sons how to do it with him. "Maybe when they're adults," he said, "they'll get into making beer, and we can make a tradition of trying out different breweries together."
- Decorating gingerbread houses and cookies is always a hit—just be sure you have a plan to let go of all the sugar-inspired energy afterward!
- One word: Play-Doh (or is that two?).

IF YOU'VE HAD A LOT OF COFFEE AND ARE EAGER TO CHALLENGE MARTHA STEWART

Yes, there may be times when you have energy and creativity running through your veins. For those times, try these activities:

- Molly loves making inventions with her five-year-old son. "In our garage," she says, "we have a huge cardboard box of crazy stuff (hooks, bungee cords, wires, sticks, pulleys, casters, cleats, binder clips, ropes, balls, buckets). We can work together to make something fun, such as hanging ropes and blankets around the garage to make a fort, making a stuffed animal 'trap' with a rope tied to a ruler propping up a laundry basket, etc."
- Lisa makes things out of the recycling with her preschooler all the time, using duct tape, stickers, crepe paper, and crayons. Cardboard and plastic bottles become a jellyfish, a fire hydrant, or a barn. In a few days, the creations go back in the recycling bin.

WHEN YOU WANT TO GO OUTSIDE, BUT PLEASE NOT TO THE PARK AGAIN!

- Go to a plant nursery and ride around in a wagon, then sniff all the flowers.

- Go to any free, outdoor concert you can find.
- Bring a picnic to a construction site and watch the action.
- Go on an "exploration" walk. See how many things you can spot: flowers, birds, trucks, colors—whatever interests you and your children. You can even take a book with images or print pictures to look for.
- Take a bike ride. You don't have to go far, and in fact you can even be on foot while your kids are riding. If one child is too little, he can go in a wagon while the bigger kid rides his bike.

WHEN THE WEATHER IS BEASTLY BUT YOU REALLY NEED TO GET OUT OF THE HOUSE

- Embrace it! Get everyone in their wellies and raincoats and splash in puddles. Run around to avoid getting too cold. Yes, you will be muddy and sopping wet, but you can make the excursion brief, then make getting warm again part of the fun.
- Lisa and her son go to a hardware store, he rides in a race-car cart, and they look at tools, some of which Lisa needs to purchase. Then they open and close every single refrigerator on display.
- Kate and her kids take public transportation for the sake of taking a ride. She lives in Oakland, California, and the commuter ferry is a big hit.
- Michael takes his son to a small-aircraft airport. They eat in the diner and watch the planes take off and land.

☑ **Do you express interest in your child's hobbies?**

When your children are young, it's fairly easy to bring them along with your hobbies, but as they get older, they will develop their own firm opinions about what they do and do not enjoy. They may not want to go hiking and camping once they turn, say, ten, preferring to spend their time playing the flute or doing something else. You may be a music fan but your son wants nothing to do with it once he gets older. Instead, he is obsessed with sports—watching them, playing them, every sport and every season! What do you do? Do you

> **EMMA TIP**
> When in doubt, just look at your child and copy whatever it is he's doing. He will love being the leader!

a. embrace sports for his sake—take him to a baseball game and ask him to explain what's going on, hiding your boredom;

b. encourage him to embrace music—take him to concerts and play Pandora in order to acclimate him more to your world; or

c. find a sport you *do* like—maybe even love—and focus on doing that together?

This is a bit of a trick question, because I'd suggest trying all of the answers. But if you really dislike baseball, don't pretend to be who you're not—that will make the time together that much harder to maintain. Absolutely still go to your *son*'s games and root him on, but that doesn't mean you also have to become a die-hard Yankee fan yourself. There's also nothing wrong with continuing to expose your son to your love of music—maybe he will love it someday—but it might also not be the best focus for your quality time together. Instead, c is the best answer—try to find a middle ground. Find something else you can do together or embrace a segment of his hobby that you will genuinely enjoy. For instance, maybe you don't love baseball but you really love taking score during games on one of those complicated scorecards. Or perhaps your daughter loves shopping, and even though you don't, you can always get in the spirit of a trip to Goodwill, which feels more like a treasure hunt. Or maybe you will have to compromise even further. Bethany's mother was very interested in sewing and quilting, as was Bethany's older sister, but Bethany never really took to it. Her mum didn't push it on her, but instead made separate efforts to do things just with Bethany, such as dinners out. And when Bethany started to knit when she was older, Bethany's mum took it up as a hobby as well.

☑ Does your family have traditions?

Traditions can be traditional or a little more irreverent. My friend Molly's family, for instance, has a little plastic turkey decoration that's about the size of a softball, and for years, the family has essentially played a game of "keep away" with it. If you have the turkey, you can't tell anyone, but you also have to try to get rid of it. So at family gatherings, everyone is paranoid that someone else is trying to slip the turkey in their suitcase or raincoat. Once the family was sitting at a restaurant, and when Molly's brother grabbed the bread-basket, instead of a roll inside he found the turkey!

A much more typical tradition comes from my friend Leslie. Each year, her family has Berry Day. They go berry picking and then make homemade berry ice cream. Berry Day goes well with Fry Fest for this food-loving family. For Fry Fest, Leslie's entire extended family gathers at a beach house with a deep-fat fryer. They began the tradition with frying fresh seafood and onions rings, but now they fry vegetables and even candy bars for an epic annual feast.

My friend Brian's family has a rustic cabin that's been around for generations called Camp Dunlookin (because when his ancestors found it, they were "done looking"). Wild blackberry pie is a frequent offering at Camp Dunlookin, and tradition holds that you can lick your pie plate when you're through, but you must do so while sitting *under* the table. Another tradition in Brian's family is Polar Bear Day, wherein on January 1 all of their friends and family gather for a dip in the freezing cold lake, followed by a hot-buttered rum (or hot chocolate for the kids). Polar Bear Day in Brian's family began in the early 1920s, and from the 1940s onward, they chronicled all of the participants in a book that sits on a shelf all year except for on Polar Bear Day. On that day, all of the "jumpers" get to write their name in the book, the water temperature and outside weather is recorded, and everyone poses for a photograph.

Jenna's family performs Christmas skits every Christmas Eve. When the tradition began, the younger generation would perform a Christmas-themed play for the grown-ups. That has since morphed so that the younger generation performs for the older generation, and *then* the older generation performs for the younger. Each year a different "Santa" appears to close the show. One year Santa was a revolving fan; another year Santa was the family's dog.

There is no right or wrong tradition, and it's fine to copy someone else's or try something out that doesn't end up "sticking." The point, rather, is that traditions are the moments that provide the glue for a family, that say you share something very important. And for children, it feels wonderful to be a part of that. For grown-ups, too.

☑ **Are you letting go of expectations and letting your child's special activities be *hers*?**

Going with the flow is the most important thing you can do when spending time with your child. Ask your child if he'd like to do a special activity, and if he wants to pitch a tent in the backyard, do it! Don't worry that it will make a mess—he can help you clean it up. The only rule one mum I know has about any activity is that they need to engage with it for longer than it takes to clean up. But that's it!

The Lego tower doesn't have to be perfect, or even good. The cookies you're making together can be strangely shaped, the blackberries you're picking can stain everyone's fingers—who cares?

If you're at Disneyland for your daughter, and she wants to stay in the princess tent, don't push her out of it because you want her to go on a dozen rides before the day's end. Follow her lead before encouraging her to explore other areas, and if you don't rush through the park and see absolutely everything, that's fine.

Disciplined Play

A friend of mine always says, "It takes discipline to play," and he's completely right. The older we get, the more difficult it becomes to use our imaginations, and it becomes close to impossible to turn off our to-do list and the "schedule" part of our brain and to really enjoy the moment. One trick I use to help bring me back to the present is to reminisce about my own childhood. I can put myself in the child's shoes by remembering

> **EMMA TIP**
>
> Try spending an entire evening with your children with no technology: no smartphone, no television, no computer time. Note what a difference it makes!

some of my fondest moments growing up. It's a way of reminding myself how important these moments feel, and how much they *mean*, to children.

Though my mum raised me and my brother on her own for much of our childhoods, and thus was very busy, she did a phenomenal job spending quality time with us, too. She was (and is!) an excellent baker—in fact, we earned some of our income by making sweet mince pies and Christmas cakes to sell at the shop down the road from our house. Every time I see one of those sweets, I'm transported back to my family kitchen with its cork floor and cream laminate counter, where my mum taught me to roll out marzipan and how to cut it. Once she even had to cut my hair because I somehow got marzipan stuck in it. Though that day wasn't exactly my favorite, I'm filled with warmth whenever I see or taste marzipan. My mum also loved to take me and my brother on long walks in the fields near our home (and we were lucky if we returned home without my accident-prone brother injuring himself). My mum was also a great swimmer and taught us how to swim. I still hear her voice in my head each time I get into a pool. A friend of mine has the same experience whenever she goes skiing. Her dad taught her how to ski, and thirty years later she still hears, "Okay, now plant your pole! Turn! Plant! Turn!" in her head each and every time she turns her skis down a mountain.

So where does this leave you if you don't have the fondest memories of childhood? If your parents didn't spend quality time with you, then think about those who did. Maybe it was a teacher, a coach, or a friend's parent. Most children have some happy memories of childhood—think about how powerful they still are, and how much they shaped you. And help create such memories for your child.

CONCLUSION

Keep Calm and Parent On

Trusting Your Instincts

At the risk of negating all of my expertise, it must be said that no one knows as much as you do when it comes to your child. I've made the argument that sometimes we are standing too close to see a problem for what it is, and that's true. But at the same time, if you receive advice that does not sit well with you—even if that advice is coming from your pediatrician—consider why that is, and then trust yourself.

For example, a friend of mine had a baby who was (and still is) very petite. The growth chart her pediatrician lived by placed the baby in the 0 percentile, and so the doctor put intense pressure on her to supplement her breast milk with formula. This advice did not ring true to my friend. This was her second baby, so she knew her milk supply well and knew the baby was latching on and feeding properly. She knew that the baby was gaining weight and hitting all of her other development markers. Yes, her baby was petite but she showed all of the other signs of perfect health. My friend trusted her instincts and didn't feel supplementing was necessary. Three years later, her daughter eats peanut butter and eggs and butter and all kinds of hearty foods, and she is still in the 0 percentile. She is simply a petite kid, and her mum knew it from the start.

You may have come across advice in this book that doesn't work for your child. Perhaps she doesn't respond to counting, or is particularly sensitive in another area. Parenting is not "one size fits all" and an approach that suits one child might be wrong for another. For instance, I sent a mum a suggested schedule when she was battling her preschooler in the morning, and it looked much like the schedule on page 152: 1. Wake up, 2. get dressed, and 3. have breakfast. Underneath this suggestion is the principle that you want the child to do the work (getting dressed) before receiving a benefit (having breakfast). The mum tried it but the battles went on. She recognized, though, that her daughter was particularly ravenous in the morning. Mum got much better cooperation from her daughter if the calories went in first thing. So she told her daughter to select her clothes the night before, then take them down to breakfast with her. The daughter was permitted to eat in her pajamas, and once she was done, she got dressed in the kitchen. Though this went against the order I usually recommend, the important thing is that it worked for this family, and mornings moved along much more smoothly.

What I've tried to do throughout this book is provide a musical bass: these are principles that work and these are common places where people get hung up. But you and your child will form the treble notes, you will have to determine the approach that works. As you do so, however, keep these tenets in mind:

Know yourself.

Remember the story about the mum who resisted her boys' behavioral diagnoses? Part of why she was able to do this was that she knew she wasn't one of those mums who thought her boys walked on water. They were imperfect beings, so it wasn't that she was trying to keep pristine images for them—she just knew that they were ultimately just normal kids who needed more productive ways to channel their energies, and she trusted that she was unbiased enough to see the situation for what it was. As a parent, know your biases. If you tend to be a bit controlling, you probably have been told this by others a time or two in your life (or a hundred). Watch that inclination, and know you may have to fight your tendencies when your kids want to wear stripes with plaids.

Know your culture.

If you are about to say "Absolutely not!" when your eight-year-old wants to go to his friend's house for a sleepover, consider whether that's *your* discomfort or your culture's. If you constantly keep processed juice in the fridge, consider whether that's actually *your* need or a cultural norm. If your child is rude to an elder and you shrug it off as "kids will be kids!" consider whether that's *your* actual view or your culture's expectation. If your six-year-old has an activity every night of the week, consider if that's *your* preference or your culture's pace. Sometimes you have to tune in to culture before you can separate your instincts from what the masses are doing, because the masses are not always right.

Know your child.

As most parents who have multiple children know, no two children can be parented exactly the same way. The principles in this book may all be helpful, but how you use them will differ. For a very sensitive child, you will use a lighter touch than with a child who really needs—even *wants*—a firm hand. For a child with more difficulty making friends, you may know that having an activity every night of the week actually makes him much happier. Your children will tell you what they need; your primary job is to be open so that you can hear.

Make exceptions.

Remember, "everything in moderation, including moderation." Do not forego a special barbecue because you're committed to a firm bedtime routine. Do not skip vacations because you fear the chaos that will come on your return. Have birthday cake, not whole-grain oatmeal, for breakfast on your child's special day. If each time your daughter comes home from ballet class she's in tears because she feels so fat and big compared to the other girls, let go of the "you committed to this! You must do it!" part of your brain, and let her bow out. And as much as I am a stickler for consistency, if your child is at her wit's end, let her apology for bad behavior wait for another time. Listen to your children, and know when—and what—to let go. It's like the tree sapling from Chapter Seven. Stake your tree and tie it, then loosen the tie as it grows. If a storm comes or the tree starts to grow in the wrong direction, tighten up.

Adapt.

If something you try doesn't work, simply course correct. The best lessons are still learned by trial and error. And what worked yesterday won't always work tomorrow. Parents particularly talk about this phenomenon when it comes to children's sleep ("Just when we'd figured out what he needed, he slid back two steps!"), but it's actually true throughout childhood. Your six-year-old may need a different approach when he's seven. Your exhausted three-year-old may need you to be ultrafirm with him one day but the next will be inordinately accommodating and sensitive, only to go back to crazy-land the following day.

Be sensible.

When you find yourself in the weeds, the trenches, or whatever metaphor best suits *those* days—everyone's up by 5:00 a.m., half the family is sick, the other half is cranky, and there's no food in the house—then stop and collect yourself. If you were an outsider, coming in and viewing the day's problems, what would you suggest? If I were perched on your shoulder like a little Jiminy Cricket, what do you think I would advise? Remove yourself as best you can and just ask what the most sensible course is for the day ahead. **Then keep calm and parent on.**

EMMA'S PARENTING REMINDERS

- Expect more from your children, and they will rise to it. Expect less, and they will sink.
- Bad behavior is a habit that can be broken.
- You need not meet your child's every need every moment he has one. Make life easier for yourself, tell him he must wait, and teach him a lesson in patience in the process.
- Don't let your child rule the roost or stop you from doing something. Know that you can handle whatever she throws your way because you are the parent, and she is the child.
- Let your child's behavior affect her, not you.
- If a child threatens a temper tantrum if she doesn't get the lolly she wants, the better parent is the one who lets the child cry rather than filling her mouth with a lolly.
- We need to be more honest about how hard parenting is.
- Having feelings of anger and frustration with your children *does not* make you a failure.
- We put loads of energy into our communication style when it comes to business and marriage, but communicating with our children requires similar attention.

- Always remember: kids *want* to please you.
- You must always know you are the parent, and your child is going to do as you say. If they don't, you will handle it. You are not afraid of him having a meltdown, because you know you'll be able to handle it.
- It is so easy to be only half-present. Don't be.
- In parenting, consistency is everything.
- The prolonged negotiations, fights, coaxing, and plain energy devoted to getting a child to eat are unnecessary. Kids will eat when they're hungry.
- Parenting by being at your child's beck and call is exhausting, and *does not* make you a better parent. Quite the contrary!
- A child is not born with manners and good values. He has to learn them, and it's a parent's job to teach them.
- Manners have everything to do with respect.
- Do not become inured to your children treating you badly. It is a very severe problem with repercussions in every area of the child's life. If your child doesn't respect you, then who and what will he respect?
- When we stop tolerating bad behavior, we raise the bar.
- Your kids aren't always going to like you, and that's okay.
- Give children plenty of room—if a behavior is not an issue of safety or respect, consider letting it go.
- Gratitude is what prevents the slippery slope to entitlement.
- Breaking routine in times of chaos will not ease your troubles or your child's—it will only add to the chaos!

- Though the first day or two of a schedule might incur a battle or two, by the end of the week, it will just happen. It's not magic, it's routine.
- Let kids be kids.
- Let go—let your children make their own choices, and experience their own consequences.
- Caving in might be easier in the short term, but is much harder in the long run.
- Children will seek attention, whether it be negative or positive.
- Kids sense when you're irritated or weak, and if there's a chance they may be able to push your buttons and get away with something or just get a reaction out of you, they will.
- Sometimes an answer is just plain "no" and it's time to move on.
- Choices empower kids, and more than almost anything else, they want to feel a sense of control over their lives.
- Instead of looking for quick fixes, pull up your socks and figure out the root of a problem.
- Letting a child take the lead in taking care of himself does wonders for building his independence and self-esteem.
- The best present is your presence, so make sure you are really and truly present.
- Always keep calm, and parent on.

CHECKLISTS

1. THE DIGNIFIED PARENT—FOR MUM AND DAD

☐ Are you getting enough sleep?

☐ Are you making time to care for yourself?

☐ Are you making time to care for your relationship with your partner?

☐ Do you greet your spouse first?

☐ Mums: Are you having sex with your partner?

☐ Dads: Are you taking care of Mum?

☐ If there are two parents at home, are you modeling a good relationship to your children in how you treat each other?

☐ Is there joy in the house? Is there a lot of laughter and fun?

☐ Do you enjoy being a parent?

☐ Do you feel confident you can handle your child's behavior?

☐ Are you calm?

☐ Do you ensure that everything does not revolve around the children?

☐ Are you forgiving of yourself when things don't go well?

☐ Are you willing to ask for help?

2. THE KING'S SPEECH—COMMUNICATION

- ☐ Are tantrums infrequent rather than often?
- ☐ Does your child listen at home as well as he does at school?
- ☐ Does your child hear and pay attention to your requests?
- ☐ Do you say the seven most important things? (I love you, I'm sorry, Yes, Stop, Please, Thank you, I know you can do it)
- ☐ Are you specific about the behavior you want, or don't want, and why? Have you explained the consequences?
- ☐ Are you communicating the behavior you want ahead of time?
- ☐ Do you avoid commands?
- ☐ Do you tell your child what to do rather than ask?
- ☐ Does your word choice place the responsibility on your child?
- ☐ Do you say it like you mean it?
- ☐ Are you avoiding tones that are too strong?
- ☐ Are you physically near your child and making eye contact when you're making a point?
- ☐ Is your body language sending a consistent message with your words?
- ☐ Are you communicating about transitions?
- ☐ If your child is very young—a baby or young toddler—do you talk to him and assume he's able to understand? Do you tell him what's happening and why?
- ☐ Are you offering choices?
- ☐ Are you using concepts and language that are age appropriate?
- ☐ Do you avoid repeating a request ad nauseam?

- ☐ Is your child able to talk to you? Do you hear her, listen to her, and respond?
- ☐ Are you reading your child's body language?
- ☐ Do you wait until your child is calm before communicating with her?
- ☐ Are you encouraging your child to use his words instead of whining or crying?
- ☐ Are the adults in your child's life consistent with one another?

3. SOLDIERING FORTH TO THE LAND OF NOD—SLEEP SECRETS

Checklist #1: The Easy Bits—Diagnosing the Problem and Setting the Scene

- ☐ Is your child behaving well?
- ☐ Is your child getting enough sleep?
- ☐ Is your child sleeping in his own bed?
- ☐ Does your child have a suitable sleep environment?
- ☐ Are you avoiding high-energy activities before sleep?
- ☐ Are you giving your child cues for sleep? Are you watching for his?
- ☐ For babies: Is your baby on a schedule?
- ☐ For kids: Is your child on a schedule?
- ☐ Is your child getting enough exercise and fresh air during the day?
- ☐ Is your child napping regularly?

Checklist #2: The Harder Bits—Habits and Expectations

- ☐ Can your child put herself to sleep? Are you avoiding "crutches"?
- ☐ Can you put your child down during the day?
- ☐ Can your child get back into his bed on his own once he gets out?
- ☐ Does your child accept when it's bedtime?
- ☐ Is your child waking up in a decent mood?
- ☐ Can you rule out nightmares?

Checklist #3: The Really Hard Bits— When the Problem Is You

- ☐ Do you allow your child to cry?
- ☐ Have you made your expectations clear?
- ☐ Do you enforce rules around sleep?
- ☐ Are you consistent?
- ☐ Are you tuned in?
- ☐ Are you ready?

4. A TALE OF PORRIDGE AND PUDDING—PROPER NUTRITION

- ☐ Do you back off if your child doesn't want to eat?
- ☐ Is your child a healthy weight?
- ☐ Does your child eat at regular intervals? Do you also avoid constant snacking?
- ☐ Does your child sit down to eat?
- ☐ Does your child have good table manners?
- ☐ Do you limit the amount of sugar in your child's diet?
- ☐ Are you offering a varied diet?
- ☐ Do you prevent your child from filling up on beverages?
- ☐ Do you avoid removing "offensive" food from your child's plate?
- ☐ Is your child aware of what he's eating?
- ☐ Are you a good role model around food and nutrition?
- ☐ Do you monitor the quality and quantity of snack food available?
- ☐ Are your expectations reasonable?
- ☐ Do you offer incentives like dessert, but not too often?
- ☐ Do you give your child a choice?
- ☐ Do you routinely introduce new foods?
- ☐ Do you persist if your child doesn't like something the first time he tries it?
- ☐ Do you avoid food games?
- ☐ Are you trusting your instincts about your child's weight?

5. LITTLE LORDS AND LADIES—MANNERS AND RESPECT

- ☐ Does your child refrain from interrupting?
- ☐ Are you developing patience in your child?
- ☐ Are you developing generosity in your child?
- ☐ Does your child ask for things properly?
- ☐ Does your child treat his things well?
- ☐ Does your child behave well around his peers?
- ☐ Does your child treat her siblings well?
- ☐ Does your child respect her elders?
- ☐ Does your child respect **you**?
- ☐ Are you clear about who's the parent?
- ☐ Does your child behave well in public settings?
- ☐ Does your child appear presentable?
- ☐ Does your child have proper mealtime manners?
- ☐ Are you teaching your child empathy?
- ☐ Does your child understand and say he's sorry?
- ☐ Do you enforce manners?
- ☐ Does your child express gratitude?
- ☐ Does your child greet people properly and say good-bye properly (or at all)?
- ☐ Are you a good role model?
- ☐ Are you polite with your children? Do you speak to them with respect?
- ☐ Do you respect your child's body?
- ☐ Are you respectful of your own things?

- ☐ Is your language appropriate?
- ☐ Do you have realistic expectations about what your child is capable of?

6. A TIME AND PLACE FOR EVERYTHING—SCHEDULING AND ROUTINES

- ☐ Does your child have a routine?
- ☐ Does your child know what that routine is?
- ☐ Does your child eat and sleep at regular intervals?
- ☐ Does your child spend enough time at home, but not too much time?
- ☐ Does your child have time to explore and use her imagination and creativity?
- ☐ Are you encouraging independent play, rather than being available at all times?
- ☐ Are focused activities part of the schedule?
- ☐ Is your child getting time outdoors?
- ☐ Is quiet time part of the schedule?
- ☐ Is active, physical time part of the schedule?
- ☐ Is your child able to focus well on activities like homework?
- ☐ Are you allowing enough transition time?
- ☐ Do playtimes and incentives follow task times?
- ☐ Are you limiting television?
- ☐ Are you limiting *all* screen time?
- ☐ Is whatever your child is watching or playing with appropriate?
- ☐ Are you flexible when you have to be?
- ☐ Are you okay with your child getting dirty, exploring, and running free (within reason)?

7. THE MAGINOT LINE—BOUNDARIES AND CONSEQUENCES

☐ Does your child hear and understand "no"?

☐ Is your child clear about what his consequences will be?

☐ Is your child given the chance to correct his behavior?

☐ Are you firm? Do you follow through?

☐ Are you making a tantrum your *child's* problem, not yours?

☐ Do you maintain a poker face when your child experiences a consequence?

☐ Are you willing to let your child be upset?

☐ Are you willing to let your child experience healthy fear?

☐ Are you supportive of teachers' and others' efforts to set boundaries and enforce consequences with your child?

☐ Are the boundaries consistent?

☐ Are *you* consistent?

☐ Do you trust your child to adhere to nonphysical boundaries?

☐ Do you let your child pick herself up when she falls?

☐ Do you hold your child accountable for her actions?

☐ Do you avoid arguing and negotiating?

☐ Are you letting your child make his own choices?

☐ Do you resist offering bribes?

☐ Are you picking your battles?

8. THE LIONHEARTED CHILD—SELF-ESTEEM

- ☐ Do you discourage clingy behavior?
- ☐ Do you avoid labels?
- ☐ Does your child have friends? Is she invited to friends' houses for playdates and birthday parties?
- ☐ Can your child cope with criticism?
- ☐ Is your child allowed to be himself? Is that good enough for you?
- ☐ Is your child liked by her teacher? Is that a good relationship?
- ☐ Do you help your child navigate his strengths and weaknesses?
- ☐ Does your child have a nervous habit like nail-biting or teeth-grinding, or complain about stomachaches?
- ☐ Is your child sad or withdrawn?
- ☐ Is your child being bullied?
- ☐ Does your child have chores and responsibilities that match her capabilities?
- ☐ Is your child allowed to complete tasks, imperfectly, on her own?
- ☐ Do you praise more than you admonish? Do you recognize when your child does something well?
- ☐ Do you avoid talking about your child's behavior in front of her?
- ☐ Do you avoid favoritism?
- ☐ Do you role model a positive/healthy self-esteem?
- ☐ Do you show love and affection daily?
- ☐ Do you react appropriately to your child's disappointment or failures?

9. QUIETING THE RABBLE—QUALITY TIME

- ☐ Do you know your child well?
- ☐ Is your child getting enough attention from each parent?
- ☐ Is your child having fun when he's with you? Are you making small moments count versus having it all be task-driven?
- ☐ Are you spending time with your child each day?
- ☐ Are you saying hello and good-bye?
- ☐ Are you truly present with your child, without a smartphone, newspaper, or other distraction?
- ☐ Are mealtimes family time?
- ☐ Do you focus on your child straightaway after an absence?
- ☐ Do you know how to be with your child?
- ☐ Do you express interest in your child's hobbies?
- ☐ Does your family have traditions?
- ☐ Are you letting go of expectations and letting your child's special activities be *hers*?

ACKNOWLEDGMENTS

Like parenting, writing a book takes a village and I've been fortunate enough to have had an incredible village throughout this project.

I've had *the* publishing dream team as I've worked on this project, for which I feel so lucky, not to mention incredibly grateful. Firstly, I'd like to thank everyone at Atria Books, including Judith Curr, Ben Lee, Kyoko Watanabe, Sarah Wright, Elaine Broeder, Hillary Tisman, and Jeanne Lee. I could not have asked for a better editor than Greer Hendricks, whose excitement, vision, and advocacy for the book made the whole process so fun and seamless. I fell in love with Greer the first time I met her and knew she was who I wanted to publish the book. When I received her offer it was truly a dream come true. Sarah Cantin's support is greatly appreciated, as is her inspired title idea.

I really couldn't have done it without my writer, Jenna Free. She has been an absolute angel throughout the entire process, helping me through every step and offering continuous support and guidance. I really owe the concept idea to Jenna. During the early stages of developing the book she asked me, "What do you do when you get called into a family's home?"

"Well," I said, "to diagnose the problem I observe the family—parents *and* children—in their home and run through a checklist."

"That's it," Jenna said. "You need to write down your checklist." She has spent hours editing pages upon pages of my notes, listening to all my stories, rants about philosophies, and, of course, my opinions on manners or lack thereof. (Yes, eating with your mouth closed and talking with your mouth full *do* constitute two different manners!)

I have the best agent, Howard Yoon. He believed in me and was passionate about the project from the start, holding my hand through all the steps. He literally took my vision and made it a reality—promising me a book deal by Christmas. Then he made it happen. Thanks, too, to his partner, Gail Ross, whose enthusiasm I keenly felt.

Martin and Jennifer Coles have been great supporters of mine for years, and offered not only a place to stay while I worked on the book but also countless hours of encouragement and guidance. They are the reason I moved to the U.S. to begin with. Martin and Jennifer brought me here as their nanny, and they have been my surrogate family ever since.

Debra Messing has likewise been a longtime champion, generously offering her time and friendship whenever I needed it. She kindly offered to write the foreword and has always been a tremendous sounding-board, providing a slew of advice and guidance. She has always pushed me to pursue my dreams and endeavors. On my first day of filming the TLC show *Take Home Nanny*, I was so nervous that Debra gave me a bottle of Rescue Remedy. She just failed to tell me I needed to drink the whole bottle!

Debra Messing and Daniel Zelman have also kindly opened their homes to me every time I visit New York for meetings. I'm incredibly grateful to you both for your continued support and a big thank-you to Roman for sharing his bedroom and giving me the bottom bunk. After all, you can't put a grown-up on the top bunk, that wouldn't show good manners!

I am very grateful to Lucinda Southworth for her support and encouragement throughout the project. Whether it was giving me the time I needed to work, reading through early drafts of the book, or promoting the book amongst her friends, Lucy's feedback and support has been invaluable.

I'd like to thank two people who really influenced a turning point in my career: Gerry McKean (Executive Producer of *Take Home Nanny*) and Julie Swales (Elizabeth Rose Agency). Thank you for pushing me outside of my comfort zone—you've opened many doors and endless opportunities.

Thank you to the many parents and friends—especially other nannies—who contributed stories, wisdom, and tips for the book. I'd also like to thank Kathy Cockerill, who spent hours helping me pull together the curriculum we teach in L.A., some of which is in this book.

I'd like to give my friends Lorraine Cronin, Silvia Klinger, Robyn Bruns, Susan Carruthers, Tobiah Roosevelt, Vaniane Schello, and Barbara LeBlanc, and my family a special thanks for putting up with me during the project. I was buried in my laptop and drafts for hours on end and asked them to listen to ideas and stories at every turn. Thank you for your patience and understanding.

A special word of thanks to Charles Jacob. Your support and patience means the world to me, as did the time you spent taking my author picture.

I'm deeply grateful to my sister, Jessica, and my uncle, Martin, for reading early drafts of the manuscript and offering helpful, thoughtful feedback. My uncle said he was blown away by the book and was surprised I knew so many words! Charming! My brother, Mark, has believed in me and my book from day one, from being a proud cheerleader to calming my nerves before important meetings to offering support and motivation throughout the entire process.

I'd like to thank my Nana. Unfortunately, she is no longer with us, but much like my mum she had very high expectations about how one should conduct oneself to be an acceptable part of society.

I spent a lot of time with my Nana during my childhood, and she really helped mold the person I am today. For that I am eternally grateful.

Last but not least, a very special word of thanks to my mum, who not only read through early drafts but provided the basis for my entire philosophy. Her parenting gave me the values, perseverance, and dedication that were essential to finishing this book. I thank her every day for the values and morals she taught me. I may not have had the best piano lessons in town but I certainly had the best mum!

INDEX

B

D

E

L

M

S

Y